Quilted Projects
with Wool *and* Wool Felt

Quilted Projects
with Wool *and* Wool Felt

Easy Techniques with Full-Size Templates

Rachel Thomas Pellman
and Beth Oberholtzer

About the Authors

"I am grateful to live in an area where weekend bike rides take me on back roads through meadows, fields, and gardens filled with animals, crops, flowers, trees, and birds. They fill my mind with beauty and color."

Rachel Thomas Pellman and her husband Kenny own and operate Rachel's of Greenfield where she designs and produces kits for small appliqué and pieced wall quilts, ornament kits, and punchneedle embroidery kits. Rachel has spent many hours in Amish homes learning the stories of Amish women, the histories of their quilts, and current trends in Amish quiltmaking. She has authored and co-authored numerous books including *Amish Wall Quilts, The World of Amish Quilts, A Treasury of Amish Quilts* and *Tips for Quilters*. Other ventures include designing several lines of fabric with P & B Textiles. She teaches and lectures at local guilds and has participated in educational programs at Sotheby's and American Folk Art Museum in New York City. Rachel grew up in Lancaster County, Pennsylvania, the youngest in a family of ten children. She graduated from Eastern Mennonite University with a degree in Home Economics education. She and Kenny happily share their lives with two sons, daughters-in-law and grandchildren. They live in Lancaster, Pennsylvania and are members of Rossmere Mennonite Church.

Beth Oberholtzer is a graphic designer, photographer, and writer from Lancaster, Pennsylvania. She co-authored two previous books: *Crazy Quilt Christmas Stockings* and *False Graining Techniques*.

ISBN 978-1-57421-727-8

Library of Congress Cataloging-in-Publication Data

Pellman, Rachel T. (Rachel Thomas)
  Quilted projects with wool and wool felt / Rachel Thomas Pellman and Beth Oberholtzer.
    pages cm
  Includes index.
  Summary: "Presents basic instructions and projects for quilting with wool and wool felt, including information on tools, fabrics, piecing, applique and binding. Features five projects with layout diagrams and cutting templates"-- Provided by publisher.
  ISBN 978-1-57421-727-8 (pbk.)
  1. Quilting--Patterns. 2. Appliqué--Patterns. 3. Wool fabrics. I. Oberholtzer, Beth. II. Title.
  TT835.P4455 2014
  746.46--dc23
                  2013021250

© 2014 by Rachel Thomas Pellman, Beth Oberholtzer, and Design Originals, www.d-originals.com, an imprint of Fox Chapel Publishing, 800-457-9112, 1970 Broad Street, East Petersburg, PA 17520.

Printed in China
First printing

CHICKEN HOT PADS 32

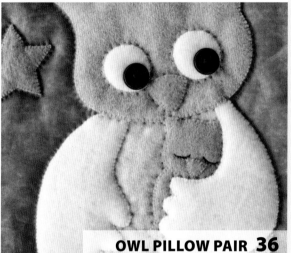

OWL PILLOW PAIR 36

MEADOW WALL QUILT 42

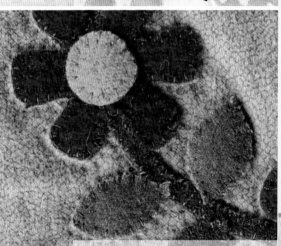

NATURE WALL QUILT 50

Contents

Part I: Tools and Techniques

Part II: Projects

Part III: Diagrams and Templates

Introduction

My earliest memory of sewing is from first grade. I remember complaining one morning that I had nothing to wear to school. I don't know what a video of the morning would show, but my memory says that my dear mother pulled out a piece of seersucker fabric, cut a front and back panel, sewed a few seams, inserted elastic to fit my waist, and sent me happily off to school wearing a brand new skirt.

Coming from a large Mennonite family, sewing was expected for my sisters and me. My mother, and later I, made most of my clothing throughout my high school years. My mom sewed my white eyelet wedding dress.

While I was very comfortable with fabric, needle, and thread, quilting didn't enter the picture for me until after graduation from college. I worked in a fabric and craft store where local people brought their wares to sell to the large tourist population that visits Lancaster County, Pennsylvania each year. Every week I encountered women (many of them Amish) who were both buying fabric for quilts and bringing finished quilts to the store to sell. I was captivated. These were gentle, unassuming craftspeople doing amazing, creative things with fabric. And though they didn't identify themselves as "artists," quilts were an outlet for their creative energy. I began to think I could do that!

Quilters are generally open to sharing ideas, techniques, and tips of the trade. I have yet to meet a quiltmaker who withholds information about how she, or sometimes he, works her magic. I am the beneficiary of a long line of quilters who imparted their wisdom without reserve. I learned tiny appliqué stitches from Emma Weaver. Dozens of Amish women who cheerfully talked with me about their memories of old quilts taught me about the deep rich colors and simple patterns of traditional Amish designs. I was amazed by the daring, unusual, and completely successful color combinations of Mildred Mast. Rosie Mutter taught me that outside-the-box quilting lines can add a whole additional dimension to pieced and appliquéd quilts. Katie Esh willingly showed me her large collection of quilting stencils and told stories of how they were used. The women in my quilt group challenged me to try tiny little patches and new techniques. Quilts exhibited in shows are an ongoing source of inspiration. Anything I know about quilting, I credit to the scores of quilters who have gone before me.

I learn best by watching. From my point of view, the easiest way to learn is to sit at the elbow of a patient, skilled crafter and watch them work. It is my hope that this book, with its pictures and text, will give you that feeling. I have tried to give enough detail and information that you will be able to follow the steps to a successful end. And while you may follow the patterns precisely as given, you should also take as much artistic license as you wish. The owl pillow blocks may be used in a wall quilt, or the sheep wall quilt block may be made into a pillow. Have fun, be creative!

The projects in the book are small. You don't have to commit a year of your life to finishing them. While my mother was a very patient seamstress, I seem to have inherited enough of my Dad's "get it done now" genes that I prefer working on projects where beginning and end come together fairly quickly. The projects in this book fit that model. While I am a firm believer in doing something carefully and well, I don't think it should take forever.

My design inspiration starts with simplicity. If it isn't simple, I can't draw it. I am grateful to live in an area where a weekend bike ride takes me on back roads through meadows, fields, and gardens filled with animals, crops, flowers, trees, and birds. They fill my mind with beauty and color.

I wouldn't have tackled this book without the prompting of my co-author, Beth, who believed we could do something to make the beauty and fun of quiltmaking accessible to everyone.

"Quilters are generally open to sharing ideas, techniques, and tips of the trade. I have yet to meet a quiltmaker who withholds information about how she, or sometimes he, works her magic."

What You'll Learn

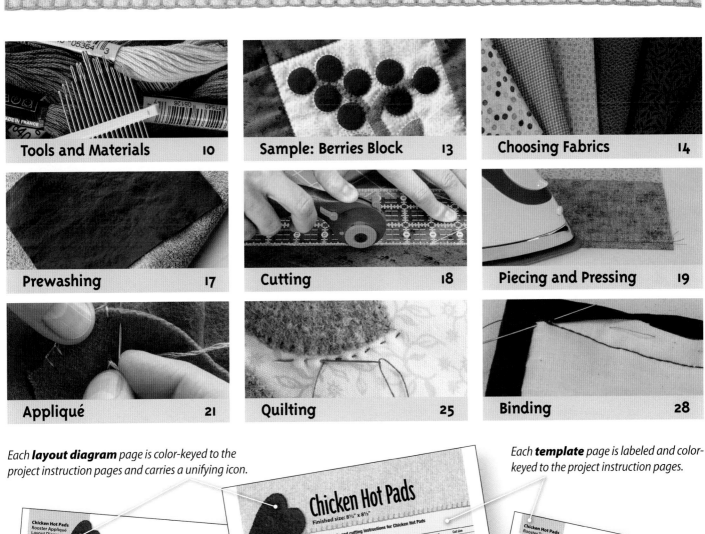

Tools and Materials	10
Sample: Berries Block	13
Choosing Fabrics	14
Prewashing	17
Cutting	18
Piecing and Pressing	19
Appliqué	21
Quilting	25
Binding	28

*Each **layout diagram** page is color-keyed to the project instruction pages and carries a unifying icon.*

*Each **template** page is labeled and color-keyed to the project instruction pages.*

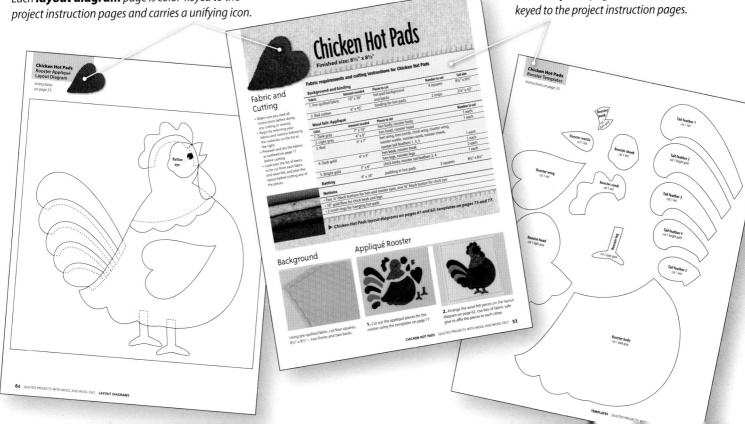

PART I
Tools and Techniques

COTTON FABRIC

Tools and Materials

APPLIQUÉ FABRIC

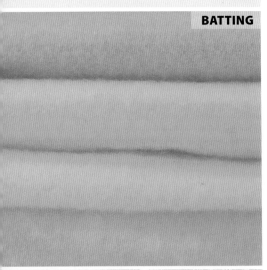

BATTING

Quiltmaking requires only the most basic elements—fabric, scissors, needles, thread, a thimble, willing hands, and a learner's mind. Early quiltmakers did fabulous work without the benefits of the newest tools, gadgets, and technologies. It can be done!

There are, however, some items that add to both efficiency and accuracy. A list of quilting items is given below. While not all are mandatory, these can enhance the quilting experience.

Fabric: High quality, 100% cotton fabrics are the traditional choice for quiltmaking. It is ideal for patchwork quilts and is a great choice for the background fabric in the projects in this book. More information on selecting fabric for projects in this book is given on page 14.

Batting: Batting choices are varied. It can be 100% polyester, 100% cotton, or a blend of the two. Wool and silk varieties are also available. Thicker batting will create a more fluffy end product and thinner batting a flatter finished piece. I prefer a low loft polyester batting. I find it easy to quilt through the batting and I like the dimension it provides when I quilt around the appliqué shapes.

Scissors: All cutting is easier and more accurate with a pair of sharp, pointed scissors. An 8- to 9-inch pair of scissors is great for cutting fabric. I also love having a tiny 4-inch pair for clipping threads.

Rotary cutter, ruler and mat: This combination of tools makes it possible to cut straight edges very accurately and efficiently. Fabric is laid on the mat and the rotary cutter blade cuts against the edge of the companion ruler. I like a 24" x 36" mat as it allows for laying out a length of 44/45" fabric (folded in half) and cutting the whole way across the fabric. The required companion for this efficient cut is a 24" ruler. I like having several additional rulers for making smaller cuts. I find many uses for my 3" x 18" and 6" x 12" rulers.

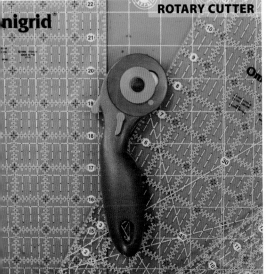

ROTARY CUTTER

SCISSORS

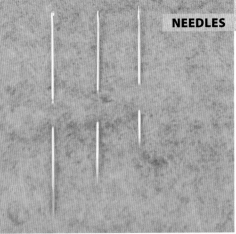

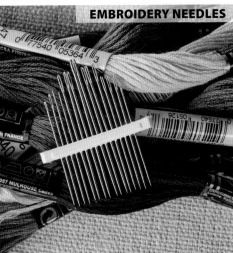

Needles: Needles come in a variety of styles for different functions. While it is possible to use the same needle for many purposes, there are some advantages to having needles designed for a specific style of stitching. The following are specific to the projects in this book.

- *Appliqué* or *Milliners* needles are fine and long and are my preference for appliqué stitching (top photo, left).
- *Sharps* are all-purpose needles used for hand sewing such as finishing a binding or sewing buttons (top photo, center).
- *Betweens* are shorter than sharps and are used for quilting (top photo, right).
- *Embroidery* needles are a bit larger with a longer threading eye to accommodate the heavier embroidery thread.

Needles are sized by number—the higher the number, the smaller the needle. I generally prefer a size 9 or 10 needle.

Thread: It is easy to be overwhelmed by thread options. I prefer to buy all-purpose sewing thread and use it for machine sewing, hand sewing, and appliqué. Embroidery floss or pearl cotton thread can be used for embroidery embellishment. Quilting thread (slightly heavier than all-purpose thread) is used for quilting.

Thimble: The beautiful silver thimbles of long ago have given way to a large assortment of shapes and styles. While I still do a lot of hand stitching (including all my appliqué) without a thimble, I find it nearly impossible to do a nice quilting stitch without one. I suggest finding a thimble that is comfortable, and learning to wear it.

Pins: Sewing accurate, precise seams is easier with the aid of pins. I like silk pins for their sharp points, small heads, and fine shafts. I love having a magnetic pin cushion for keeping them all in place!

If you have difficulty seeing the eye of the needle when threading, hold it in front of something white. The white ground will make it easier to see the opening.

TOOLS AND MATERIALS QUILTED PROJECTS WITH WOOL AND WOOL FELT **11**

PENS & PENCILS

Quilting frame: A quilting frame plays the important role of keeping the three layers of the quilt flat while quilting. Frames can be as simple as a quilting hoop (which looks like a very large embroidery hoop) or an elaborate frame with separate rails for stretching each layer of the quilt. My personal favorite is a square hoop on a floor frame. The floor frame supports the hoop for me and it turns so that I can quilt in any direction.

Light: Being able to see is a huge boost to both the ease and quality of your work. A good light source makes it easier to thread needles, and great visibility increases the accuracy of all your stitches.

Sewing machine: A basic machine with straight stitching will do the trick. A reliable, consistent machine greatly enhances the sewing process. Stitch length should be set so there are about 12 to 14 stitches per inch. While slower, it is also possible to do all stitching neatly and accurately by hand.

QUILTING HOOPS

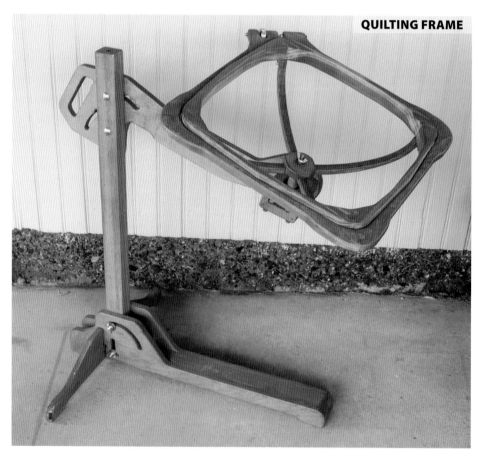

QUILTING FRAME

Marking pens/pencils: Projects in this book will require tracing onto wool felt (such as WoolFelt® brand) or wool. A fine line marker or pen will work well for tracing the templates on wool felt. Wool should be backed with a fusible web material, and a pencil or pen can be used to trace the templates onto the fusible web paper backing.

Buttons: Buttons are used for eyes in the projects in this book. The size and color needed are listed on the requirements chart. As an alternative to a wool or wool felt appliqué, bright, colorful buttons can also be substituted for flower centers or berries.

BUTTONS

Sample: Berries Block

The following pages detail the techniques you will use when making an appliquéd quilt project. As an example, the Berries Block has been used to show construction, appliqué, quilting, and binding on pages 13 to 29. I show the block finished with binding; however, I also offer the option of framing it for hanging on page 95.

Here are the steps you will follow for the Berries Block as well as the projects that begin on page 30.

1. Read all instructions before beginning.
2. Choose background fabrics.
3. Choose appliqué fabrics.
4. Prewash fabrics.
5. Look over the list of items to be cut from each fabric and wool felt, and plan the layout before cutting any of the pieces.
6. Cut background and border fabrics.
7. Piece and press background and border fabrics.

8. Iron fusible web stabilizer onto appliqué fabric if necessary.
9. Trace and cut appliqué shapes.
10. Appliqué pieces onto background.
11. Add embellishments.
12. Layer backing, batting, and quilt top in preparation for quilting.
13. Quilt the fabric "sandwich."
14. Add binding.
15. Sign and date your handiwork.

▶ *Berries Block layout diagram on page 72; templates on page 93.*

How to Read the Fabric Requirements and Cutting Instructions Charts

Total amount of each fabric color you need.

Carefully plan how the pieces can be arranged to make the best use of your fabric.

The "cut size" is a bit smaller than the "amount needed" to allow for any uneven edges and ensure adequate fabric.

General fabric colors are listed. Specifics depend on the look you want.

You'll be directed to pages with the appropriate templates.

How many pieces you'll cut from each template.

Batting you need is listed after the fabric.

Fabric requirements and cutting instructions for Berries Block

Cotton fabric

Color	Amount needed	Pieces to cut	Number to cut	Cut size
1. Beige	approx. 8" x 8"	background	1 square	6½" x 6½"
2. Dark green	approx. 8" x 13"	borders	4	3" x 6½"
3. Dark red	approx. 12" x 18"	corner blocks	4	3" x 3"
		binding strips	2	2" x 18"
4. Beige solid	14" x 14" backing	use whole piece, then trim to size		

Appliqué: Wool felt

Color	Amount needed	Pieces to cut	Number to cut
1. Green	4½" x 6"	berry stem	1
		leaves	3
2. Red	2½" x 5"	berries	8
Batting	14" x14"	inner layer	trim to size after quilting is completed

Choosing Fabrics

Choosing Fabrics for Backgrounds

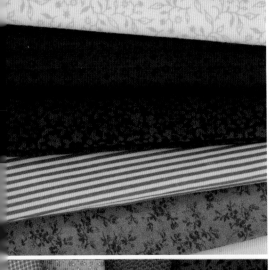

The standard fabrics for traditional quiltmaking are tightly woven, plain weave, high quality 100% cottons. The fabrics you buy should look good and they should also feel good in your hands.

It is OK to use re-purposed fabrics (fabrics salvaged from old clothing, etc) in quiltmaking if they are on par with the other fabrics with which they will be used. They should be comparable in weight and durability.

Of course, one always has artistic license, and fabrics of any type and texture may be combined. Keep in mind that fabrics of very different styles may present more of a challenge when sewing them together.

Background fabrics for the projects in this book include cottons, cotton flannels, and pre-quilted fabric for the hot pads.

Fabric selection includes the fun of color choices. The goal is to have fabrics that coordinate, complement, and contrast. Contrasting and/or complementary fabrics for different patches will give definition to the design while allowing all the patches to blend into a compatible whole.

Sashing strips divide background patches most effectively when they contrast with the background fabrics. Backgrounds may be printed or solid colored fabrics. Variety in color, visual texture, scale, and proportion adds interest For instance, if you decide to use beige for background fabrics, choose beiges with varying color values and different prints to create visual interest. You may want to combine stripes with dots or flowered prints with geometrics.

Keep the appliqué designs in mind when choosing the background, and choose fabrics that will highlight and not compete with the appliqué motifs.

 Fabric colors will create the mood of your project. Very bright, bold colors will set a playful, dramatic mood. Colors that are more muted establish a sedate, calm feeling.

*I chose rich red, olive green, and beige cotton prints, above left, for the border and background of my **berries block**. The heather green and red wool felt I selected, above right, nicely complement the cotton prints chosen for the background.*

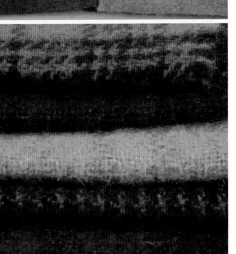

Choosing Fabrics for Appliqué

When choosing colors for the appliqués, be sure there is enough contrast so the appliqué image pops from the background fabric. Colors that are too similar will be lost when viewed from a distance. This is also true when layering appliqué on appliqué. Even when you want a shape to appear as largely one unit and one color, contrast will be interesting.

The appliqué shapes in this book are applied without turning under any seam allowances. Since that is the case, *only* fabrics that will not fray along the cut edges are suitable for appliqué projects in this book. Examples of such fabrics are felted wools, wool felt, bamboo felt, felt made from recycled fibers, sturdy fleece, and other fabrics that will not fray when cut.

The appliqués in the projects shown throughout this book are made with felted wool, wool felt, and fleece. Selections were made based on texture and color. Important considerations are that the fabrics not fray, and that they are compatible with the end use of the project.

Wool felt is the name for a wool/polyester blend material in which fibers are blended, compacted, and pressed. This process creates a smooth, dense material with tangled fibers that will not fray when cut. WoolFelt® is a trademark brand of wood felt, and is my preferred product and the brand of wool felt used throughout this book. Other types of sturdy felt made from bamboo or recycled materials may also be used as long as they are will not fray. Be sure any felt product used for appliqué shapes feels sturdy and durable. I do not recommend the use of lightweight craft felt.

Wool felt is not the same as felted wool. Felted wool is 100% wool that has been felted. Felting may be done using wool fibers that are squeezed and pressed into a flat, compact fabric, or it may be made by shrinking woven wool fabric. The wool used for the Nature Wall Quilt in this book is woven wool fabric that has been felted. The felting process happens when hot water and agitation open the little barbs in the wool fibers and allow them to interlock and shrink together. While most of the shrinkage is done with water and agitation, it also helps to dry the wet wool fabric in a dryer. The woven fabric becomes a more dense, compact material. This tight wool can be cut into appliqué shapes without frayed edges. Felting can be done with woven wool fabric, knitted wool sweaters, and blankets.

If wool fabric has been treated during manufacture of the fabric to make it "washable wool," it will not shrink and is not suitable for felting.

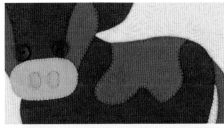

If you want a totally brown Jersey cow, use browns with enough variety to create a noticeably shaded brown cow. When doing a pumpkin, shading can be subtle but should still have enough contrast to define the shapes.

The top two photos at the left show a variety of wool felt options available for your appliqués. The third photo from the top shows several rich colors and weaves available in felted wool. A variety of recycled felted wool is shown in the photo at the bottom left.

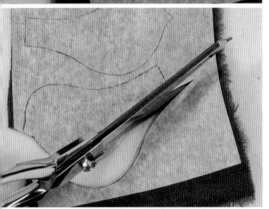

Iron-on Webbing to Stabilize Edges

Properly felted woven wool fabrics will fray very little when cut. However, to maintain edges that are crisp and smooth, I use an iron-on fusible web stabilizer on the back side of all wool appliqués. I use it on all appliqués, but it is especially important on small shapes or narrow stems where stitching may pull threads along the edge and make the shape unstable.

You will need to stitch through the fusible web after it has been adhered to the background fabric, so it is important to choose webbing that results in a lightweight and flexible bond.

Follow manufactures instructions and fuse the webbing to the wrong side of the appliqué shapes prior to cutting. Products like Steam-A-Seam® or HeatnBond® Lite have paper backing which is great for tracing the shapes. Mistyfuse® does not have a paper backing, but has the advantage of producing a very flexible, lightweight bond. It can be ironed onto parchment paper (available in grocery stores near foil and waxed paper) to create a paper back for tracing.

I recommend placing a silicone pressing sheet (nothing will stick to it) between the iron and the fusible web appliqués to protect your iron from stray adhesive.

This fusible web backing on the appliqués assures clean edges, and also provides an adhesive bond to the background fabric. When pressed in place, stitching around the edges would not be necessary. I prefer to see stitching around the edges of all the appliqué shapes and for that reason, I stitch around all the appliqués even though the stitching is mainly decorative.

I do not use fusible web on the back of wool felt, bamboo felt, or fleece appliqués.

It is a good idea to prewash and dry any fabrics that will be used in quiltmaking—especially if the finished project will be washed in the future. Prewashing will take care of shrinkage and will also tell you if the colors in the fabric will bleed or run when wet. Instructions for prewashing cotton fabrics are different from those for wool or wool felt.

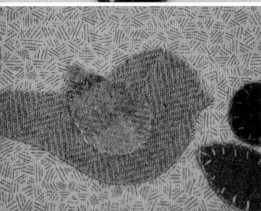

Prewashing

Prewashing Cotton

Fabrics should be washed, dried, and ironed prior to use in quiltmaking. While any fabric may bleed, dark, intense colors are the most vulnerable. Wash then alone or with like colors until there is no color loss. Drying in a dryer will help to pre-shrink any fabric that has a shrinkage tendency.

In addition to removing excess fabric dyes, prewashing will remove sizing added to fabrics in the manufacturing process to make them feel crisp and smooth. This loss of sizing makes the fabrics more soft and pliable. To bring back the crisp, smooth texture, give the washed and dried fabrics a light squirt of spray starch before ironing them. The starched, pressed fabric is now ready for cutting and piecing. The revived crispness is helpful in achieving accuracy in both cutting and sewing.

If you are using cotton flannels or any other fabric with a "brushed" finish, place a towel on the ironing surface and lay the fabric, right side down, on the towel before ironing. The texture of the towel will help to preserve the texture of the brushed finish on the fabric.

Prewashing Wool

If you buy felted wool, it will not need to be washed before using it for appliqués. It has been washed in the felting process. If you prefer to do your own felting, see page 16 for directions. Felting wool is essentially shrinking it until it is tightly locked together and none of the woven threads will separate from each other.

Prewashing Wool Felt

Prewashing of wool felt for the appliqué shapes is important for both shrinkage and color bleeding. Prewashing of the wool felt will give it a softer, slightly pebbly texture. It can be ironed to bring back a partially or totally smooth finish.

It is very common to have color bleeding from the wool felt. For that reason, it is important to wash colors separately to avoid color transfer from piece to piece. Prewashing will also decrease the chances of color transfer after the project is completed.

Before prewashing, wool felt is smooth (above left). The texture of wool felt that has been prewashed is rumpled (above center). You may use the coarser textured wool felt or make it smooth again by ironing.

How to Prewash Wool Felt

1. Fill a sink or dishpan with warm water and add a drop of dish detergent. Immerse the wool felt and allow it to soak until saturated. Swish the wool felt in the water to gently agitate the fibers. Repeat the process until the color bleeding stops.

2. Lift the piece from the water and squeeze gently to remove most of the moisture. Avoid twisting and creasing the wool felt.

3. If the pieces are small, lay them flat on a towel to dry. Large pieces may be placed in a dryer with an old towel (which may absorb color from the wool felt). Dry similar colors together. Wipe out the dryer after use, or dry an old towel, to be sure no color is left to transfer to your next load of clothes!

 If you choose to wash the finished item, wash it in cold water, and dry it flat or line dry. You may also want to use a commercially-produced color catcher to decrease dye migration.

Cutting

Precision in cutting is the first step in accurate piecing. The rotary cutting system (mat, ruler, cutter) increases accuracy and precision. It does take some getting used to, so you may want to do a bit of practice with some scrap fabric. The ruler is held in place with one hand while the cutter glides along the edge of the ruler with the other hand. It is important to hold the ruler firmly so there is no shifting or sliding as the cutter rolls along the ruler's edge. When cutting long strips, stop occasionally to change the position of your hand on the ruler, or walk the hand holding the ruler alongside the cutter so the ruler does not move as the cutter pressure against it progresses. The blade on the cutter is extremely sharp! Always use caution, cut away from yourself, and keep fingers away from the blade.

If you do not have a rotary cutter, scissors will do. When cutting by hand, mark lines onto the fabric and cut on the lines. There are a variety of fabric marking pencils available. Chalk shows well on dark fabrics and a lead pencil works well on light fabrics. Choose a marking tool that will not bleed out into the fabric.

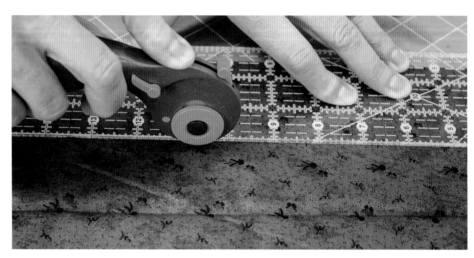

A rotary cutter system, above, helps you cut fabric quickly, smoothly, and accurately.

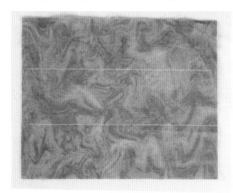

When cutting by hand, mark lines, then cut on the marked lines.

 Look over the list of items to be cut from each fabric, and plan the layout before cutting the pieces. As a general rule, larger pieces should be cut first and then smaller pieces.

Fabric Grain

The lengthwise and crosswise weave, visible in the back of this fabric, is the grain. If you cut with the grain the piece will have more stability than if you cut at an angle.

*Here are the cut borders, corners, and background for my **berries block**. See the fabric requirements and cutting instructions for the berries block on page 13.*

Piecing and Pressing

"Piecing" is the term used for sewing pieces, or patches, of fabric together. Patches are laid, right sides together, and stitched in place. The standard quilting seam allowance for pieced patches is ¼". There should be exactly ¼" from the edge of the fabric to the seam line. It is very important to maintain an accurate ¼" seam allowance consistently throughout the process. Any variation in the seam allowance will show up as uneven lines and as corners that will not meet in clean, precise joints. Check your seam allowance regularly for accuracy.

Piecing can be done by hand or with a sewing machine. One of the advantages of hand piecing is accuracy. The pace of hand sewing allows you to place each stitch precisely and carefully. Another advantage is portability. Patches that are pinned together can easily be carried on road trips, to appointments, long games, etc. When hand piecing, stitches need to be small and tight, creating smooth, flat seams. When piecing by hand, the seam line is often marked with a pencil to assure straight, accurate stitching.

The seam at the top was stitched by hand. Compare that with the vertical seam that was sewn by machine.

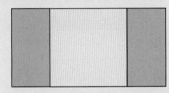

Background Assembly for the Berries Block

1. Sew a border to each side of the background patch. Press seams toward borders.

2. Sew a corner block to each end of the two remaining borders. Press seams toward borders.

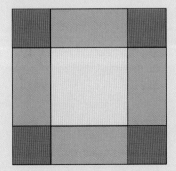

3. Sew a border/corner block unit to each side of the background patch. Press seams toward borders.

Press As You Piece

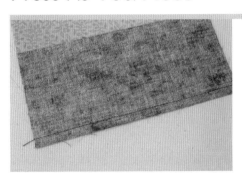

1. There should be exactly ¼" from the edge of the fabric to the seam line. It is very important to maintain an accurate ¼" seam allowance consistently throughout the process.

2. After the seam is sewn, use a dry iron (no steam) to press it flat. This sets the stitches. Press gently, being careful not to stretch or distort the seam.

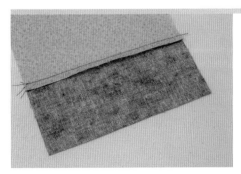

3. Press the seam to the right or left, depending on how it will join the next unit. Pressing direction is given with the assembly instructions for each project.

4. Piece together the border and background fabrics in the order given in the assembly instructions, pressing as you go. Here two corner blocks are sewn to a border.

Press As You Piece (continued)

5. Sew the corner blocks to the top and bottom borders

6. Sew the pieced sections together, making sure to butt seams against each other at the intersections of seams.

7. Note here that the seams were pressed in opposite directions, as described in the background assembly instructions.

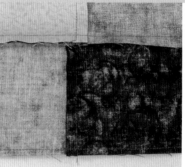

Pressing directions are given with the background assembly instructions. Note that the seam allowances here (above left) are pressed away from the center block. That way you can avoid quilting through the additional thickness when you outline the borders later (right).

8. Stitch around the outer edge of the combined patch using a ⅛" seam allowance.

How to Make and Use Thread Bunnies

I begin and end my machine stitching with little fabric scraps called thread bunnies. To make thread bunnies, cut two scraps about 1½" x 2", then fold each scrap in half so you have a ¾" x 2" rectangle.

Using thread bunnies makes feeding patches easier and eliminates tails on each individual patch since all the thread tails end up on the scraps.

1. Stitch through the thread bunny, and then feed the patches into the presser foot.

2. When you get to the end of the last patch, feed a second thread bunny into the presser foot.

3. After you've stopped the stitching on the thread bunny, cut it off and reuse it for the next series of patches.

Appliqué

Preparing the Appliqué Shapes

Templates for appliqué shapes are given in their actual size.

Cut out the paper template shapes. Be sure the shape is facing the right direction and trace it onto the appropriate appliqué material. Trace using a pen or fine point marker that will not bleed into the material. Using a sharp pair of scissors to increase accuracy, cut out the appliqué shapes. Cut on the inside edge of the marked line so no ink will be visible on the finished piece.

When tracing onto paper-backed fusible webbing, remember that the shape will be *reversed* when it is cut and place the templates appropriately.

Appliqué Placement

1. Use the appliqué layout diagrams to determine the proper placement of the appliqué shapes. Shapes can be laid directly onto the layout diagrams.

2. Use fabric safe glue and a toothpick to apply very small dots of glue where wool felt pieces overlap. The shapes can be partially or totally assembled (like a puzzle) before being pinned and stitched onto the fabric background.

3. Press down gently with your finger to glue the shapes together. Take care not to glue the pieces to the paper.

4. Use as little glue as possible since large areas of glue are difficult to stitch through and may be obvious when stitching is completed.

5. When the appliqué "puzzle" has been assembled, move it to the proper position on the background patch and pin or fuse it in place for stitching.

When assembling a shape that has been backed with fusible webbing, a light touch of the iron can hold the shape together at strategic points so it can be moved to the background patch. Be careful not to fuse it to the paper!

Appliqué Stitching

Appliqué may be done using a basic appliqué stitch or a more decorative blanket stitch. Be alert to the appliqué sequence so that overlapping shapes are applied in the proper order. Where one appliqué section overlaps another, it is not necessary to stitch the section being overlapped, as it will be held in place when the overlapping piece is stitched.

Basic Appliqué Stitch

Appliqué stitching is done with regular sewing thread. Choose a thread color to match the shape being stitched.

Appliqué stitches are tiny and catch the edge of the appliqué shape. It is important that the stitches extend into the material at least ⅟₁₆" to ⅛" so they do not pull out of the edge. Stitches should be even in both length and spacing. The needle goes through the background fabric making a stitch about ⅛" long. It re-emerges to catch the appliqué shape along the cut edge. Stitches should be tight but not so taut as to create puckers.

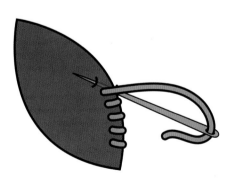

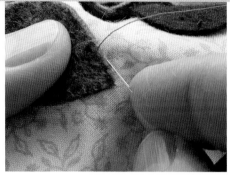

1. The appliqué stitch is worked from right to left. The needle enters the background fabric at the edge of the appliqué shape, and straight out from the last stitch. The needle is angled toward the appliqué shape so that the tip will emerge just inside the edge of the appliqué shape.

2. The tip of the needle re-emerges just inside the edge of the appliqué shape along the cut edge.

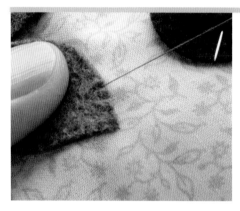

3. The appliqué stitch is finished by pulling the thread tight. The next stitch will begin straight out from the thread.

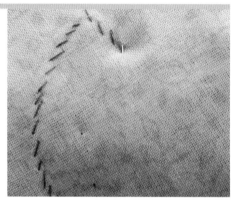

4. Continue stitching around the shape. The appliqué stitches are at right angles to the appliqué shape on the top and angled underneath.

Where appliqué overlaps (leaves over stem, for example), you need only stitch the top layer.

 Pinning the shapes from the back rather than the front avoids having the thread snag on the pins while stitching.

Appliqué Stitching (continued)

Blanket Stitch

An alterative to the basic appliqué stitch is to attach the appliqué shapes with a blanket stitch. The blanket stitch should be done with embroidery floss or pearl cotton thread. If using embroidery floss, separate the 6-strand floss and stitch using only 2 strands at a time. Thread color can either match or contrast with the color of the appliqué shape.

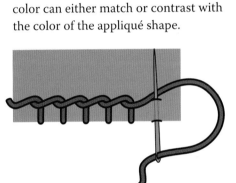

1. The blanket stitch is worked from left to right. Insert the needle into the appliqué shape about ⅛" from the edge. This point determines the size of the stitch.

2. Push the needle through the appliqué shape and the background fabric, having the tip of the needle emerge at the edge of the appliqué shape.

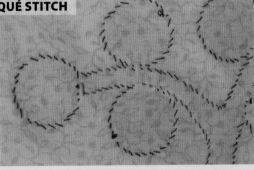

3. The needle crosses over the thread—thread underneath, needle on top.

4. Pull the stitch tight. The thread is locked on the left side of the stitch and creates an outline along the edge of the appliqué shape.

BASIC APPLIQUÉ STITCH

BLANKET STITCH

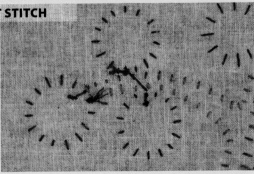

Stitch Comparison

The top two photos at the left show the front and back view of berries that have been appliquéd with the basic appliqué stitch. These stiches are very small and lend a subtle dimension. The blanket stitch, shown front and back in the bottom two photos, is larger and more decorative.

Embellishments

When your appliqué is completed, use embroidery floss (separate 6-strand floss and stitch using 2 strands of floss) or pearl cotton thread to stitch embellishments like leaf veins or pumpkin tendrils shown on the appliqué layout diagrams.

Buttons are available in a wide variety of sizes and colors. When you attach the eye buttons, follow the appliqué layout diagrams and place them with great care.

Curly embroidered tendrils bring depth and contrast to this rich pumpkin patch.

Embroidery threads can be chosen to contrast with or complement the background fabric and appliqué pieces. Other embellishment choices, such as special buttons, make each project unique.

A subtle embroidered nose and mouth, shiny black button eyes, and lovely embroidered swirls on his wooly coat add charm to this sweet sheep.

Watch Out for Goofy Eyes!
When you place the eye buttons, be aware that small variations in position can greatly affect the expression and personality of your critter. I've placed the mama owl's eyes (below) so she is watching over her baby.

Quilting

A quilt is a decorative fabric "sandwich" with three layers—top, middle, and back. The top is usually a pieced or appliquéd design. The back is a printed or plain fabric. The middle layer is batting which provides both insulation and puffiness. The three layers of the sandwich are held together by stitches that pierce through all the layers and hold them together. These stitches are the quilting stitches.

The quilting stitch is a small running stitch that pierces through all the layers of the quilt "sandwich," holding them together.

On all the projects in this book, quilting lines follow the outline of the appliqué shapes and the edges of the pieced blocks, sashing, and borders. Since the shapes serve as your guide, you will not need to mark quilting lines.

Stitch around each appliqué shape, staying close to the edge of the appliqué. Quilt along the edges of the pieced blocks, sashing, and borders.

If you wish to have more decorative quilting on your piece, you can mark additional designs on your quilt top. Options might be to add a design inside the oval of the flower block on the Nature quilt, or to quilt additional stars around the owls on the pillows. Mark the designs very lightly so they are nearly invisible under the quilting stitches, or use a quilt marking pencil that will allow for the lines to be easily removed when quilting is completed.

Use a quilting hoop or small quilting frame, as shown at the right, to keep the quilt smooth while quilting.

All the projects shown in this book have been hand quilted, but quilting can also be done by machine.

Quilting Preparation

1. To prepare for quilting, lay the quilt back, wrong side facing up, on a smooth, flat surface. Layer the batting over the quilt back. Place the quilt top, right side up, over the batting.

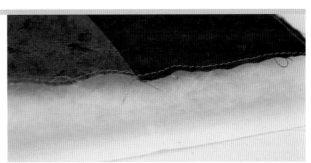

2. The batting and backing should extend slightly beyond the edges of the quilt top on all sides. Be sure all the layers are smooth and free of wrinkles.

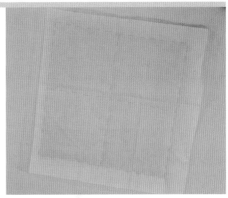

3. Baste the layers together with large stitches to prevent any shifting of the layers during the quilting process.

4. Baste from the center out to the edges in 2" to 3" intervals. Baste very close to the edge of the quilt top around the perimeter of the quilt.

The edges of a quilt wrap around the bottom of the quilting frame. The top of the frame gently clamps the quilt in place.

Quilt Stitching

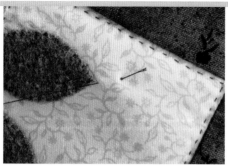

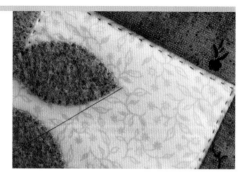

1. Begin with a small quilting needle and a single strand of quilting thread. Make a knot at the end of the thread. Insert the needle through the quilt top only at a point about ½" from where stitching will begin.

2. Have the needle emerge at the point of the first quilting stitch.The first stitch here will be right along the edge of the appliquéd leaf. The knot at the end of the thread is still visible on the surface of the fabric.

3. Gently tug on the knot until it pops under the quilt top and is lodged in the layers of the quilt.

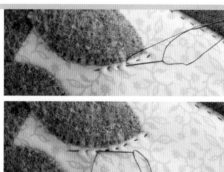

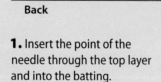

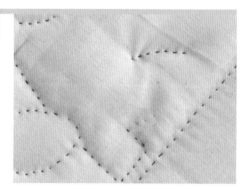

4. Use an up and down rocking motion of the needle to make small, even stitches. Be sure the needle pierces all the way through the three layers of the quilt.

5. Several stitches may be stacked on the needle at one time.

6. Quilting should be equally beautiful on the back side of the quilt. The goal is to have small, even stitches on both the front and back. This is achieved with practice.

Quilting Needle Travels

CROSS SECTION

Top
Batting
Back

You can move from one section of quilt stitching to another section of stitching by having the quilting needle travel through the batting.

If it is only a short distance, push the point of the needle through the quilt top only, and have it reemerge at the point you wish to resume stitching.

If it is a more distant point, you can travel a 2–4 inches in the following manner without having to break the quilting and re-knot the thread.

1. Insert the point of the needle through the top layer and into the batting.

2. Push the needle through the batting one needle's length. Have the point of the needle emerge, keeping the eye submerged in the batting.

3. Grasp the point of the needle and turn the eye in the batting so the eye of the needle heads in the direction you wish to travel.

4. Push the needle, eye first, through the batting one needle's length. Have the eye emerge, keeping the point submerged in the batting.

5. Grasp the eye and turn the needle again so the point heads in the direction you wish to travel.

6. Repeat turning and rotating as often as needed to get to the new quilting location.

Quilt Stitching (continued)

Outline all appliqué shapes with quilting stitches. Stitch very close to the edges of the appliqué pieces. This will make them puff a bit and will give a dimensional effect to the appliqué shapes. Quilting through multiple layers of wool or wool felt may be a challenge. In these areas it may be necessary to use "stab" stitches. Stab the needle straight down through all layers and then back up doing a single stitch at a time.

Quilt along each side of the inner borders and the quilt sashing. When outlining borders and sashing, quilt on the side away from the pressed seam allowance to avoid stitching through the additional thickness.

Quilting thread color may blend into or contrast with the color of the fabric being stitched. Contrasting thread will make the stitches much more visible. If you are new to quilting you may want to start with a thread that recedes into the background. With practice, quilting stitches are small and even.

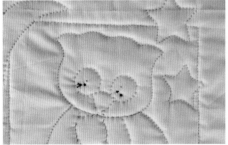

Quilting stitches go through the entire quilt sandwich (top, batting, and back), pulling the three layers together. The large, dark stitches at the owl's eyes are stitches through the buttons. I like to stitch through the buttons again after the quilting is completed to sink the buttons into the batting.

How to Make a Magic Knot!

A tiny, tight knot makes it easier to pop the knot through the quilt top.

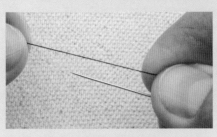

1. Thread the needle. Bring the long end of the thread parallel to the needle, with the end of the thread at the needle eye.

2. Pinch the end of the thread against the needle eye. Using the opposite hand, pinch the thread, wrap the thread around the shank of the needle at least three times (more wraps make a larger knot, fewer wrap makes a smaller knot).

3. Using the hand that did the wrapping, pinch the wrapped thread to the needle. Hold the wraps firmly in place.

4. With the opposite hand, grab the point of the needle and pull the needle and thread through the wraps.

5. Slide the entire length of the thread though the wraps.

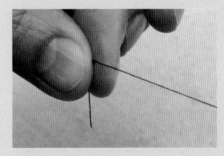

6. The wraps will form a small knot at the end of the thread.

 The eye of the needle is punched in the manufacturing process. If you have trouble threading, turn the needle around. The thread may go in more easily from the other side.

Binding

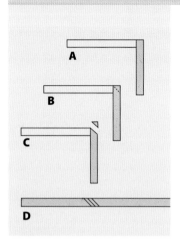

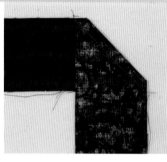

1. Place two binding strips, right sides together, with the ends at right angles to each other (A).

2. Sew the binding strips together on the diagonal from the top left corner of the top strip to the bottom right corner of the underneath strip. (B).

3. Trim away the excess corner leaving a ¼" seam allowance (C).

4. Open the strip and press the seam open (D).

5. Repeat, adding the remaining binding strips to form one long strip.

6. Fold each end of the long strip at a 45° angle and trim, leaving a ¼" seam allowance.

7. Fold the binding in half lengthwise, wrong sides together. Press.

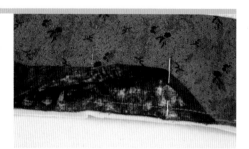

8. Carefully trim excess backing and batting from the edges of the quilt, keeping edges straight and square.

9. Beginning at the bottom edge, near the center, place the binding along the edge of the quilt top with the raw edges of the binding even with the raw edge of the quilt top. The folded edge of the binding faces the center of the quilt.

10. When starting, stitch only the bottom layer of the binding, keeping the top layer of the binding unstitched for two inches. This opening in the binding provides a place to tuck the opposite end of the binding at the finish. After two inches, stitch the binding in place through all thicknesses.

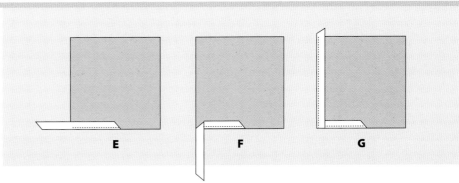

E   F   G

11. When approaching a corner, stitch to within ¼" of the corner. Stop stitching (E).

12. Fold the binding down to form a 45° angle (F).

13. Fold the binding up on itself to create the corner and align the binding with the next edge of the quilt. Begin stitching at the corner and stitch through all layers (G).

14. Rotate the quilt and continue attaching the binding along the next edge and repeat the procedure at the next corner. Continue until all corners are completed.

15. When the binding extends all the way to the starting point, cut off any excess, being very careful to leave enough to tuck inside the folded binding at the start.

16. Tuck the tail inside, align all edges, and stitch through all layers to the beginning stitching.

17. Fold the binding around to the back of the quilt, encasing the raw edges. The fold of the binding covers the stitching line on the back side of the quilt. Hand stitch the binding in place.

18. Fold the binding at the corners to create mitered corners.

19. Make several small stitches in the fold of each miter and the seam where the binding ends to tack them in place.

20. Continue hand stitching the binding all the way around the edges.

21. Remove all basting stitches from your quilt. Sign and date it using embroidery, quilting stitches, or a pen with permanent ink. I like to print the copy on my computer, trace it onto a piece of muslin, and appliqué it to the back of the quilt.

Hanging Your Quilt

There are multiple ways to hang a quilt. A rod pocket, small rings, or thread loops can be sewn to the back of the quilt, allowing for the insertion of a hidden or decorative rod. Pins or small tacks can be used for temporary hanging.

PART II
Projects

I have done my best to give detailed instructions so that all projects in the book are accessible for beginning quilters. I want you to be successful! If you are more advanced, you may skip over what you already know.

Patterns and cutting instructions are specific to each project. However, I know that quilters are a creative bunch, and I want you to feel free to adapt and adjust as you wish.

I've done my hot pads with a chicken and rooster. But if you want fruit in your kitchen, the pumpkin and the pears pattern from the Nature Quilt would be a beautiful hot pad pair. If you prefer a sheep, feel free to adjust the background size of your hot pad and use the sheep pattern from the Meadow Quilt. I like the owls as pillows, but pair the blocks vertically or horizontally and they could be a very cute wall quilt. The Nature Quilt patches could be used to make coordinating pillows.

You get the idea! I've given you detailed patterns and instructions, but you also have our blessing to branch out and experiment.

This plump chicken family will
decorate your kitchen and protect
your hands while you bake!

Chicken Hot Pads

Finished size: 8½" x 8½"

Fabric and Cutting

- Make sure you read all instructions before doing any cutting or sewing.
- Begin by selecting your fabrics and notions following the materials on the list at the right.
- Prewash and dry the fabrics as outlined on page 17 before cutting.
- Look over the list of items to be cut from each fabric and wool felt, and plan the layout before cutting any of the pieces.

Fabric requirements and cutting instructions for Chicken Hot Pads

Background and binding

Fabric	Amount needed	Pieces to cut	Number to cut	Cut size
1. Pre-quilted fabric	10" x 36"	hot pad background and backs	4 squares	8½" x 8½"
2. Red cotton	6" x 45"	binding for hot pads	2 strips	2¼" x 42"

Wool felt: Appliqué

Color	Amount needed	Pieces to cut	Number to cut
1. Dark gray	7" x 10"	hen body, rooster body	1 each
2. Light gray	4" x 6"	hen head, rooster head	1 each
3. Red	6" x 7"	hen wing, hen comb, chick wing, rooster wing, rooster wattle, rooster comb, rooster cheek, rooster tail feathers 1, 3, 5	1 each
4. Dark gold	4" x 5"	hen beak, rooster beak	1 each
		hen legs, rooster legs	2 each
5. Bright gold	3" x 6"	chick body, rooster tail feathers 2, 4	1 each
Batting	9" x 18"	padding in hot pads	2 squares	8½" x 8½"

Notions

- Two ¼" black buttons for hen and rooster eyes, one ⅛" black button for chick eye
- 18" gold floss for chick beak and legs
- 2 small rings for hanging hot pads

▶ *Chicken Hot Pads layout diagrams on pages 61 and 62; templates on pages 75 and 77.*

Background

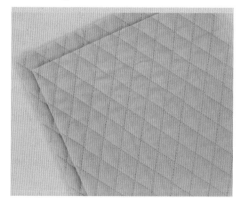

Using pre-quilted fabric, cut four squares, 8½" x 8½"—two fronts and two backs.

Appliqué Rooster

1. Cut out the appliqué pieces for the rooster using the templates on page 77.

2. Arrange the wool felt pieces on the layout diagram on page 62. Use bits of fabric-safe glue to affix the pieces to each other.

Appliqué Rooster (continued)

3. Carefully lift the partially assembled rooster onto the right side of one of the squares. Center the rooster on the square as shown on the layout diagram.

4. Stitch the rooster pieces in place on the background square. Use a single strand of regular sewing thread in a color that matches the piece being attached.

5. When appliqué is complete, sew the rooster's button eye in place.

Appliqué Hen & Chick

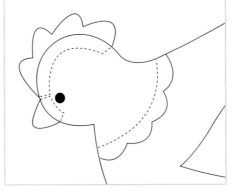

1. Cut out the appliqué pieces for the hen and chick using the templates on page 75.

2. Refer to the dashed lines on the layout diagram on page 61 to determine which sections of cut shapes are under other pieces.

3. Arrange the wool felt pieces on the layout diagram. Use bits of fabric-safe glue to affix the pieces to each other.

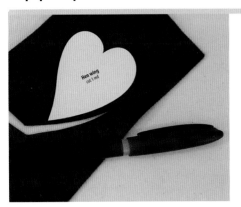

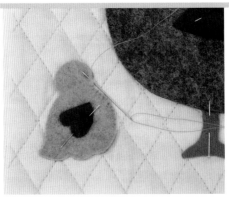

4. Carefully lift the assembled hen and chick onto the right side of one of the squares. Center the pair on the square as shown on the layout diagram.

5. Pin the pieces in place on the background square, then appliqué the edges.

6. Use a single strand of regular sewing thread in a color that matches the piece being attached.

Appliqué Hen & Chick (continued)

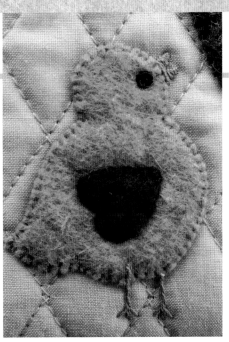

7. When the appliqué is complete, sew the hen and chick's button eyes in place. Separate 6-strand embroidery floss and use 2 strands to stitch the chick beak and legs.

8. Use a satin stitch for the chick beak and a straight stitch for the legs. This completes the front of the hot pads.

Assembly and Binding

1. Lay the hot pad backs, wrong side up, on a flat surface. Lay the batting on top of the back. Place the fronts, right side up, on top of the batting to make a sandwich of the pre-quilted squares and the batting squares.

2. Refer to the binding section on pages 28–29 for instructions on attaching the binding to the edges of the hot pad. Use one binding strip for each hot pad.

3. Turn the binding to the back side of the hot pads and hand stitch in place, making neatly folded miters at each corner on both the front and back of the hot pad.

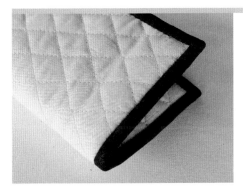

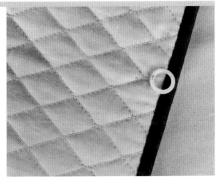

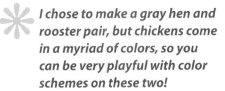

4. Fold one hot pad in half to find the center at the top of the back.

5. Sew the small hanging ring in place. Sew a ring on the other hot pad also.

I chose to make a gray hen and rooster pair, but chickens come in a myriad of colors, so you can be very playful with color schemes on these two!

This mama owl shelters her little one for peaceful slumber while two others keep watch from a nearby tree.

Owl Pillow Pair

Finished size: 14" x 14"

Fabric and Cutting

- Make sure you read all instructions before doing any cutting or sewing.
- Begin by selecting your fabrics and notions following the materials on the list at the right.
- Prewash and dry the fabrics as outlined on page 17 before cutting.
- Look over the list of items to be cut from each fabric and wool felt, and plan the layout before cutting any of the pieces.

Fabric requirements and cutting instructions for the Owl Pillow Pair

Cotton fabric: background, border, back, and binding

Color	Amount needed	Pieces to cut	Number to cut	Cut size
1. Dark blue print	12" x 24"	backgrounds	2 squares	10½" x 10½"
2. Dark brown print	12" x 27"	side borders	4	2½" x 10½"
		top and bottom borders	4	2½" x 14½"
3. Black fabric	4" x 4"	tree hole	1	3" x 3½"
4. Dark print or solid	¾ yard	pillow backs	4	14½" x 11"
5. Dark print or solid	⅓ yard	binding strips	4 strips	2½" x 36"

Wool felt: Appliqué

Color	Amount needed	Pieces to cut	Number to cut
1. Sandstone	5" x 7"	mama owl head	1
2. Oatmeal	6" x 8"	mama owl body, small owl body	1 each
3. Brown	8" x 10"	tree	1
4. Gold	8" x 8"	moon, large star, small star, mama owl foot, small owl foot; small owl beak	2 each
		mama owl beak, baby owl beak	1 each
5. Cream	6" x 8"	mama owl right wing and left wing	1 each
		mama owl eye	2
		small owl eye	4
6. Putty	4" x 5"	baby owl body, small owl head, small owl in tree	1 each
7. Camel	3" x 4"	baby owl head, small owl bib	1 each
8. Light green	3" x 5"	leaves	4
9. Dark green	3" x 4"	leaves	3

Batting	two 16" x 16"	inner layer	trim to size after quilting is completed

Notions

- Four ⁵⁄₁₆" buttons for small owl eyes, two ¾" black buttons for mama owl eyes
- 12" 6-strand black embroidery floss
- Two 14" pillow forms

▶ *Owl Pillow Pair layout diagrams on pages 63 and 64; templates on pages 79 and 81.*

Background Assembly

Sew backgrounds and borders together before doing any of the appliqué. Sew all seams using an exact ¼" seam allowance. Follow the diagrams given and sew the pieces together in the sequence shown.

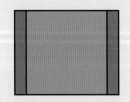
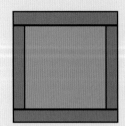

1. For each pillow top, sew a side border (2½" x 10½") to each side of the background square (10½" x 10½"). Press seams toward borders.

2. Sew a border (2½" x 14½") to the top and to the bottom of each background/border unit. Press seams toward borders.

3. Stitch around the outer edge of each top using a ⅛" seam allowance. This stitching will stabilize the edges and prevent fraying during the appliqué process.

Appliqué Tree Owls

Layout Reference

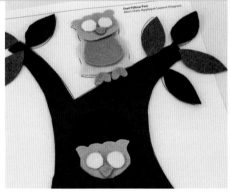

1. Cut out the appliqué pieces for the tree owls using the templates on page 81.

2. Assemble the pieces on the layout diagram on page 64. Position the leaves on the tree branches as indicated. Some of the leaves will extend beyond the edge of the page.

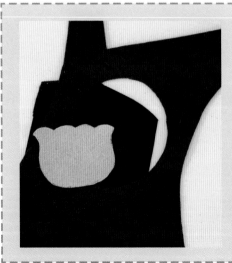

Hole in the Tree

1. Cut out the "hole in tree" paper template.
2. Position the template on the tree trunk.
3. Trace around the template.
4. Cut the hole in the tree trunk.
5. Position the tree on the background.
6. Insert black fabric behind the hole; trim away any excess fabric that sticks out beyond the tree trunk.
7. Tuck the owl into the hole.
8. Stitch the owl and the edges of the hole, stitching through black fabric onto the background.

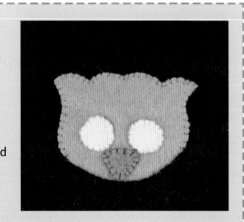

Appliqué Tree Owls (continued)

3. After using bits of fabric-safe glue to affix the pieces to each other, carefully place the assembled grouping on a background piece.

4. Refer to the diagram on page 38 to see where the moon and stars should be positioned. Pin the wool felt pieces onto the background square and stitch in place. Use a single strand of regular sewing thread that matches the piece being attached.

5. As you assemble the shapes, note the sequence so that the overlapping shapes are placed in the proper order.

6. After neatly stitching all tree owl pieces in place, position and sew on the eye buttons. Be careful when positioning the eye buttons so that the effect is what you want (see page 24).

Appliqué Mama & Baby

Layout Reference

1. Cut out the appliqué pieces for the mama and baby using the templates on pages 79. The star and moon templates are on page 81.

2. Lay the wool felt pieces on the layout diagram. Use bits of fabric-safe glue to affix the pieces to each other.

Appliqué Mama & Baby (continued)

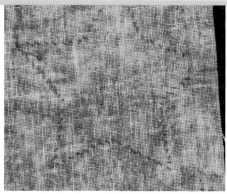

3. Refer to the layout reference on page 39 to see where the moon and stars should be positioned. Pin the wool felt pieces onto the background square and appliqué in place.

4. As this back view shows, appliqué in small, even stitches. Use a single strand of regular sewing thread in a color that matches the piece being attached.

5. When appliqué is completed, embroider the baby owl's eyes and sew button eyes on the mama owl.

Quilting

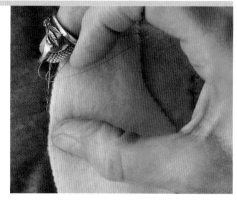

1. To prepare for quilting, layer the top, batting, and backing together for one of the pillows. Baste the layers together as shown on page 25.

2. When you quilt, use an up and down rocking motion of the needle to make small, even stitches. Be sure the needle pierces all the way through the three layers of the quilt.

3. Several stitches may be stacked on the needle at one time.

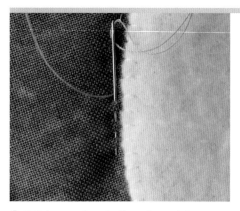

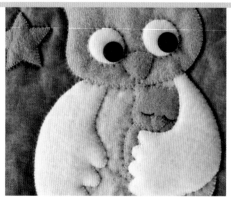

4. Stitch very close to the edges of the appliqué pieces. This will make them puff a bit and will give a dimensional effect to the shapes.

5. Quilt around the inside of the border and outline the appliqué shapes with quilting stitches.

6. Repeat steps 1 through 5 for the second pillow.

Pillow Backing and Binding

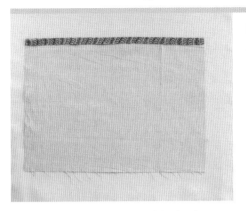

1. Select one of the pieces of the backing fabric and turn under ½" along 14½" edge of backing. Press.

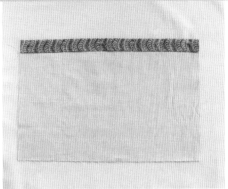

2. Turn the edge under an additional inch. Press, pin, and stitch using thread to match the backing fabric. Repeat with a second piece of backing fabric.

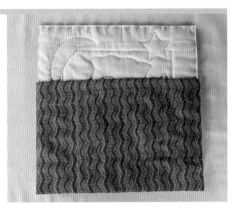

3. Lay the pillow top, wrong side up, on a smooth, flat surface. Place one backing piece on the pillow top. The right side of the fabric should be facing up and the sewn seam should be toward the center of the pillow.

4. Repeat steps 1 through 3 with the second backing piece. The backing pieces will overlap each other in the middle of the pillow. Pin the layers together and stitch around the edge of the pillow using a ¼" seam allowance.

5. Using 2 binding strips for each pillow, follow the binding instructions on page 28.

6. Wrap the binding neatly around the back and hand stitch it to both pieces of backing. Make sure your stitching is sturdy at the edges of the opening for the pillow.

7. Repeat steps 1 through 6 to create the backing and add the binding to the second pillow cover.

8. Gently insert the pillow forms into the pillow covers, being sure to tuck the corners of the pillow form into the corners of the pillow covers.

9. The generous fabric overlap neatly encloses the pillow form and keeps it in place.

Meadow Wall Quilt

Finished size: 17½" x 33"

Fabric and Cutting

- Make sure you read all instructions before doing any cutting or sewing.
- Begin by selecting your fabrics and notions following the materials on the list at the right.
- Prewash and dry the fabrics as outlined on page 17 before cutting.
- Look over the list of items to be cut from each fabric and wool felt, and plan the layout before cutting any of the pieces.

Fabric requirements and cutting instructions for Meadow Wall Quilt

Cotton fabric: background, sashing, borders, back, and binding

Color	Amount needed	Pieces to cut	Number to cut	Cut size
1. Beige print A	10" x 12"	cow background patch	1	8½" x 10"
2. Beige print B	10" x 22"	sheep background patch	1	8½" x 10"
		corner blocks	4	4" x 4"
3. Beige print C	10" x 12"	chicken background patch	1	8½" x 10"
4. Brown solid	12" x 36"	sashing strips	2 strips	1" x 10"
		top and bottom inner borders	2 strips	1" x 10"
		side inner borders	2 strips	1" x 26½"
		binding	4 strips	2" x 33"
5. Brown print	15" x 30"	top and bottom outer borders	2 strips	4" x 11"
		side outer borders	2 strips	4" x 26½"
6. Beige solid	22" x 40"	quilt back	use whole piece of fabric and trim to size after quilting is completed	

Wool felt: Appliqué

Color	Amount needed	Pieces to cut	Number to cut
1. Chestnut brown	7" x 10"	cow body, face stripe, tail tip	1 each
		cow ears	2
2. Rusty brown	6" x 8"	cow head, legs, tail, spot	1 each
3. Wheat brown	3" x 4"	cow nose, udder	1 each
		cow horns	2
4. Oatmeal	7" x 8"	sheep body	1
5. Dark gray	4" x 6"	sheep face	1
		sheep ears	2
		sheep legs	4
6. White	3" x 5"	sheep head	1
7. Red	12" x 12"	heart on sheep, chicken wing, chicken comb	1 each
		border hearts, border flowers	4 each
8. Medium gray	4" x 5"	chicken head	1
9. Light gray	7" x 9"	chicken body	1
10. Gold	5" x 6"	chicken beak	1
		chicken legs	2
		flower centers	4
11. Green	15" x 15"	long stems, ¼" x 14" strips	4
		short stems, ¼" x 6" strips	4
		leaves	36
Batting	22" x 40"	inner layer	trim to size after quilting is completed

Notions

- Two ½" buttons for cow eyes, two ⅜" buttons for sheep eyes, one ¼" button for chicken eye
- 12" tan embroidery floss for cow, 36" medium gray embroidery floss for sheep (Separate 6-strand floss and use 2 strands of floss for all stitching.)

▶ *Meadow Wall Quilt layout diagrams on pages 65–68; templates on pages 83–87.*

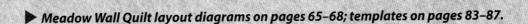

Background Assembly

Sew background and borders together before doing any of the appliqué. Sew all seams using an exact ¼" seam allowance. Follow the diagrams given and sew the pieces together in the sequence shown.

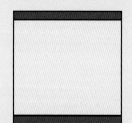

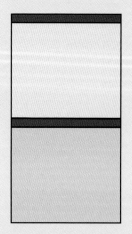

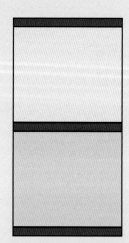

1. Select the beige cow background rectangle (8½" x 10"). Sew a solid brown inner border strip (1" x 10") to the top of the background rectangle. Press seam toward inner border.

2. Sew a solid brown sashing strip (1" x 10") to the bottom of the cow background block. Press seam toward sashing strip.

3. Select the beige sheep background rectangle (8½" x 10"). Sew it to the bottom of the sashing strip. Press seam toward sashing strip.

4. Sew a solid brown sashing strip (1" x 10") to the bottom of the sheep background block. Press seam toward sashing strip.

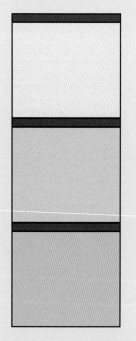

5. Select the beige chicken background rectangle (8½" x 10"). Sew it to the bottom of sashing strip. Press seam toward sashing strip.

6. Sew a solid brown inner border strip (1" x 10") to the bottom of the chicken background. Press seam toward inner border.

7. Sew a solid brown inner border strip (1" x 26½") to each side of the combined patches. Press seams toward inner borders.

8. Sew an outer border strip (4" x 26½") to each side of the combined patches. Press seams toward inner borders.

Appliqué Cow

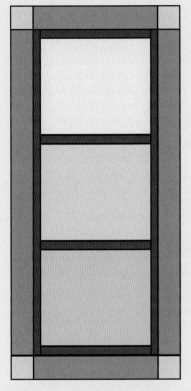

9. Sew a corner block (4" x 4") to each end of the remaining outer border strips (4" x 11"). Press seams toward borders.

10. Sew an outer border/corner block unit to the top and bottom of the combined patches. Press seams toward inner borders.

1. Cut out the appliqué pieces for the cow using the templates on page 83.

2. Assemble the wool felt pieces on the cow layout diagram on page 65. After using bits of fabric-safe glue to affix the pieces to each other, carefully place the assembled cow on its background piece.

3. Appliqué the cow pieces in place on the background square. Use a single strand of regular sewing thread in a color that matches the piece being attached.

4. After completing the appliqué stitching, shown here from the back, embroider the cow's nostrils and add the eye buttons as the diagram shows.

Layout Reference

Appliqué Sheep

1. Cut out the appliqué pieces for the sheep using the templates on page 85.

2. Assemble the wool felt pieces on the sheep layout diagram on page 66. After using bits of fabric-safe glue to affix the pieces to each other, carefully place the assembled sheep on its background piece.

3. Appliqué the sheep pieces in place on the background square. Use a single strand of regular sewing thread in a color that matches the piece being attached. Embroider the nose, mouth, and curls as the diagram shows. Add the eye buttons.

Appliqué Chicken

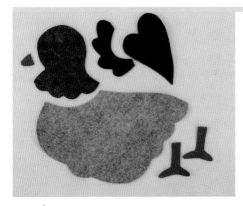

1. Cut out the appliqué pieces for the chicken using the templates on page 87.

2. Assemble the wool felt pieces on the chicken layout diagram on page 67. After using bits of fabric-safe glue to affix the pieces to each other, carefully place the assembled chicken on its background piece.

3. Pin the appliqué shapes in place on the background square. Appliqué the chicken pieces in place on the background square. Use a single strand of regular sewing thread in a color that matches the piece being attached.

4. Make your appliqué stitches small. They should be even in both length and spacing.

5. When all appliqué stitching is completed, sew the eye button in place. Refer to the chicken layout diagram on page 67 if needed.

Appliqué Border Top and Bottom

1. The drawing above shows a reduced view of the top and bottom borders. Each border will use 2 flowers, 2 flower centers, 1 heart, 6 leaves, and 2 stems cut from the templates on page 85. Each stem should be cut ¼" x 6". Use the layout diagram on page 68 or refer to the drawing above to position the pieces on the top and bottom borders.

2. Center the stems on the borders, remembering to allow for the loss of a ¼" seam allowance along the outside edges.

3. Position the stems so that each end is tucked under the center heart and the corner flower.

4. Position the leaves along the stems using the drawing as reference.

5. Pin the wool felt pieces in place on the background, then appliqué them in place.

Appliqué Border Sides

1. The drawing above shows a reduced view of the side borders. Each border will use 2 flowers, 2 flower centers, 1 heart, 12 leaves, and 2 stems cut from the templates on page 85. Each stem should be cut ¼" x 14".

2. Center the stems on the borders, remembering to allow for the loss of a ¼" seam allowance along the outside edges.

3. Position stems so that each end is tucked under the center heart and the corner flower.

4. Position the leaves, heart, and flowers relative to the stems, using the drawing as reference.

5. Pin the wool felt pieces in place on the background, then appliqué them in place.

Quilting

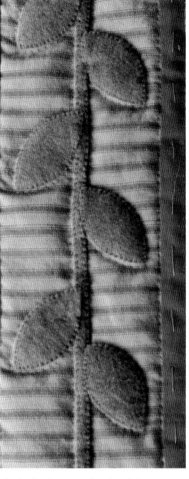

1. To prepare for quilting, layer the top, batting, and backing together. Baste the layers together as shown on page 25.

2. Follow quilting instructions on page 25. Quilt around the appliqué shapes with quilting stitches.

3. Stitch very close to the edges of the appliqué pieces. This will make them puff a bit and will give a dimensional effect to the appliqué shapes.

4. Quilt along each side of the inner borders and the quilt sashing. Remove the large basting stitches (visible on the inner border at the right) when the quilting is completed.

Binding

Refer to the binding section on pages 28–29 for instructions on how to piece together the binding and attach it to finish the edges of the Meadow Wall Quilt.

Firm But Not Tense

While you want your quilt to be held firmly in a quilting frame while you are stitching, avoid stretching it too hard. It is easier to quilt if there is a bit of flex in the quilt. There should be equal tension in the quilt top and back so there are no ripples developing as the quilting progresses. I like to start in the middle and work out to the borders, being very careful to maintain straight borders and sashing as I move out to the edges. If, when you get to the edges of the quilt you no longer have enough fabric for the edges of the frame to grab, you can pin a towel to the quilt edge to extend it.

Nature Wall Quilt

Finished size: 28" x 28"

The texture and color saturation of the 100% wool appliqué fabric add a warm glow to this rich wall quilt.

Fabric and Cutting

- Make sure you read all instructions before doing any cutting or sewing.
- Begin by selecting your fabrics and notions following the materials on the list at the right.
- Prewash and dry the fabrics as outlined on page 17 before cutting.
- Look over the list of items to be cut from each fabric and wool, and plan the layout before cutting any of the pieces.

Fabric requirements and cutting instructions for Nature Wall Quilt

Cotton fabric: background, sashing, borders, back, and binding

Color	Amount needed	Pieces to cut	Number to cut	Cut size
1. Taupe print	10" x 13"	oval flowers background	1	11½" x 9"
2. Gray print 1	12" x 20"	oak leaves backgound	1	11½" x 9"
		pumpkin background	1	6½" x 6½"
3. Gray print 2	½ yard	berries background	1	6½" x 6½"
		outer borders	4	4½" x 20½"
4. Gray solid	11" x 16"	pears background	1	6½" x 4½"
		corner blocks	4	4½" x 4½"
5. Red	½ yard	inner borders	2	1½" x 20½"
		inner borders	2	1½" x 18½"
		sashing	1	1½" x 18½"
		sashing	1	1½" x 11½"
		sashing	2	1½" x 6½"
		binding	3	2½" x 41"
6. Any color	1 yard	quilt back	1	34" x 34"

Felted wool: Appliqué

Color	Amount needed	Pieces to cut	Number to cut
1. Green Note: If you wish to have varied shades of leaves, buy a light and a dark green.	12" x 18"	oak leaf oval, oval stem, berry stem, pear leaf, pumpkin leaf	1 each
		center border berry stems	4
		corner border stems	8
		all block and border leaves	63
2. Medium red	8" x 12"	round flowers, border flowers	4 each
		border berries	12
3. Dark red	3" x 5"	berries	8
4. Light gold	6" x 8"	acorn tops	4
		round flower centers, border flower centers	4 each
		pear B	1
5. Dark gold	5" x 7"	pear A	1
		bird wings	8
6. Light orange	6" x 6"	oak leaf	2
		pumpkin front	1
7. Medium orange	10" x 12"	birds	8
		oak leaf	2
		pumpkin middle	1
8. Dark orange	4" x 6"	pumpkin back	1
9. Dark brown	3" x 4"	acorn base	4
		pear stems	2
		pumpkin stem	1
Batting	34" x 34"	inner layer	trim to size after quilting is completed

Notions

- Eight ⅛" buttons for bird eyes
- 1 yard fusible webbing
- 18" green embroidery floss for pumpkin and pear stems.
  (Separate 6-strand floss and use 2 strands of floss for all stitching.)

▶ *Nature Wall Quilt layout diagrams on pages 69–74; templates on pages 89–93.*

Background Assembly

Sew background and borders together before doing any of the appliqué. Sew all seams using an exact ¼" seam allowance. Follow the diagrams given and sew the pieces together in the sequence shown.

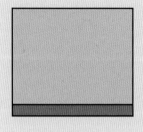

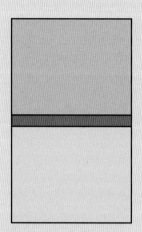

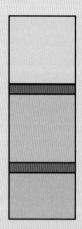

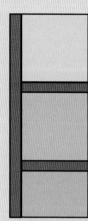

1. Select the oval flowers background rectangle (11½" x 9") and a sashing strip (1½" x 11½"). Sew the sashing strip to the bottom of the oval flower background. Press the seam toward the sashing.

2. Select the oak leaves background (11½" x 9"). Sew it to the bottom of the oval flowers/sashing unit. Press the seam toward the sashing.

3. Select the pumpkin and berries background blocks (6½" x 6½"), the pears background block (6½" x 4½"), and two sashing strips (1½" x 6½"). Begin with the pumpkin background and add a sashing strip, the berries background, sashing strip, and pears background as shown. Press all seams toward sashing.

4. Select a sashing strip (1½" x 18½") and sew it to the left side of the pumpkin/berries/pears background. Press the seam toward the sashing.

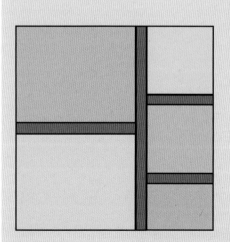

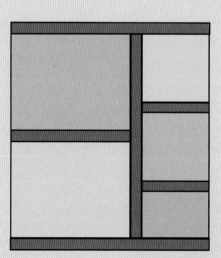

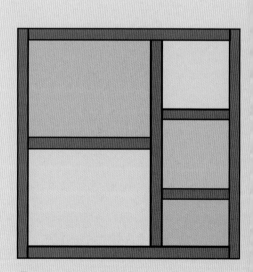

5. Sew the oval flowers/oak leaves background unit to the pumpkin/berries/pears background unit. Press the seam toward the sashing.

6. Sew an inner border strip (1½" x 18½") to the top and bottom of the background unit. Press the seams toward the inner borders.

7. Sew an inner border strip (1½" x 20½") to each side of the background unit. Press the seams toward the inner borders.

Background Assembly (continued)

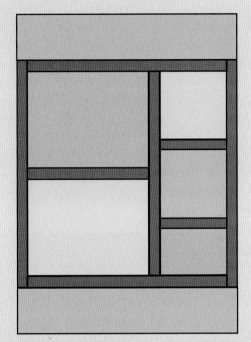

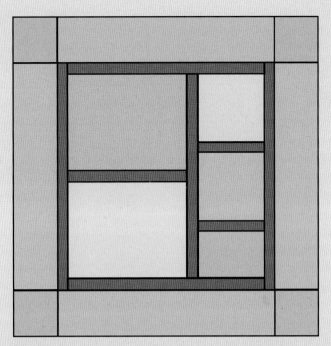

8. Sew an outer border strip (4½" x 20½") to the top and bottom of the background unit. Press the seams toward the inner borders.

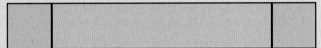

9. Sew a corner block (4½" x 4½") to each side of the remaining outer border strips (4½" x 20½"). Press the seams toward the corner blocks.

10. Sew the border/corner block unit to each side of the background. Press seams toward inner borders. Stitch around the entire outer edge of the quilt top using a ⅛" seam allowance. This stitching will stabilize the edge of the quilt and help to prevent fraying and stretching during the appliqué process.

Appliqué Oval Flowers

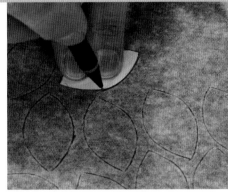

1. If you choose to use felted wool as I have, apply iron-on fusible web stabilizer to the back side of all appliqué fabric.

2. Cut out the paper templates on page 89 and trace them onto the paper backed fusible webbing which has been ironed onto the back side of the wool fabric. Remember that the shapes will be reversed when you cut them out, so trace them accordingly!

3. Cut out the appliqué shapes and peel away the paper backing so they are ready to be fused. The cost of wool fabric makes me want to use it very efficiently. I used the center of the oval stem to trace all the leaves.

Appliqué Oval Flowers (continued)

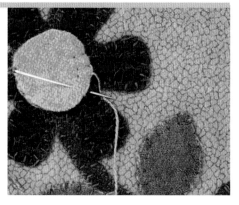

4. Use the appliqué placement diagram on page 69 as a reference for placing the wool pieces on the background. A very light touch of the iron can be used to help hold the pieces together. Be very careful not to fuse the pieces to the paper layout diagram.

5. Carefully place the oval flower pieces on the background block, making sure the unit is centered. An easy way to find the center is to fold the block in half one way and then in half again. Use your finger to lightly press a crease. The crease lines are helpful in positioning the appliqué pieces.

6. Fuse the shapes in place and then appliqué them with a decorative blanket stitch (see page 23 for instructions on the blanket stitch). Use embroidery floss (2 strands) or pearl cotton thread for stitching. The thread may match or contrast with the color of the appliqué shape.

Cutting Out the Oval Stem

Because the oval stem is so narrow, it can easily become unstable when cut. If using wool, it is important to use a fusible web stabilizer under the stem. Iron it onto the wool before tracing and cutting. Wool felt does not require the use of a fusible web stabilizer. For either material, use the cutting tips given here.

1. Cut *only* the outer edge of the paper oval template and trace it onto the wool felt or the paper-backed fusible web.

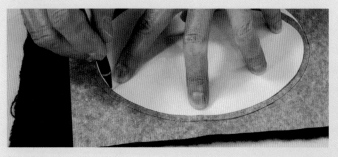

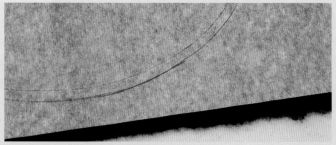

2. Next, cut the inner edge of the paper oval. Place the smaller oval inside the traced line and trace the inner line.

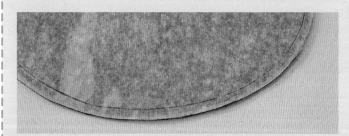

3. When cutting the wool or wool felt, cut the outside line first, and then the inner line.

Appliqué Remaining Blocks

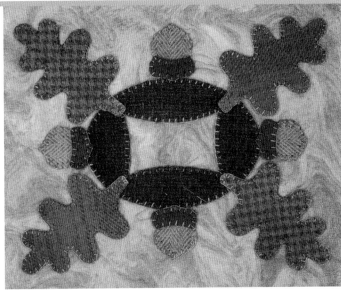

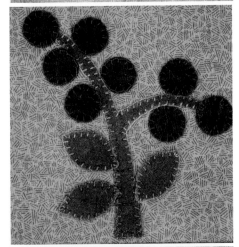

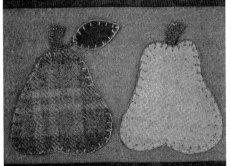

Layout Reference

Follow steps 2 through 6 for the remaining blocks: oak leaves, pumpkin, berries and pears. Center each assemblage on its background fabric block as the above layout reference shows.

When all appliqué stitching is complete, embroider the pumpkin and pear stems.

Appliqué Border

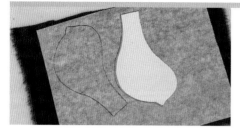

1. Cut out the paper templates on page 93 and trace the shapes onto the wool fabric. Assemble the pieces on the layout diagrams on pages 73 and 74. Half the birds and bird wings will need to be traced facing one direction and the other half facing the opposite direction.

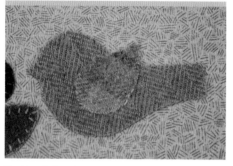

2. Carefully place the assembled units on the borders and corner backgrounds. Make sure you center each on the background fabric as the layout reference shows.

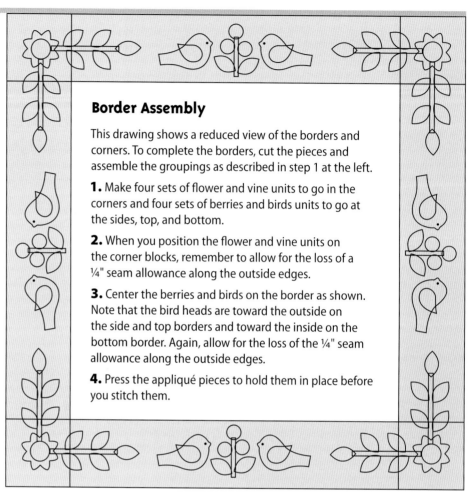

Border Assembly

This drawing shows a reduced view of the borders and corners. To complete the borders, cut the pieces and assemble the groupings as described in step 1 at the left.

1. Make four sets of flower and vine units to go in the corners and four sets of berries and birds units to go at the sides, top, and bottom.

2. When you position the flower and vine units on the corner blocks, remember to allow for the loss of a ¼" seam allowance along the outside edges.

3. Center the berries and birds on the border as shown. Note that the bird heads are toward the outside on the side and top borders and toward the inside on the bottom border. Again, allow for the loss of the ¼" seam allowance along the outside edges.

4. Press the appliqué pieces to hold them in place before you stitch them.

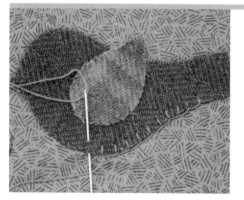

3. Appliqué the pieces in place with embroidery floss or pearl cotton thread.

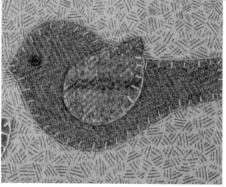

4. After your appliqué stitching is complete, sew the ⅛" eye buttons in place.

5. The back of the piece shows small, neat blanket stitches that are evenly spaced around each appliqué shape.

Quilting

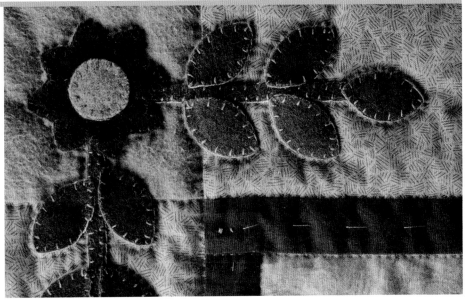

1. To prepare for quilting, layer the top, batting, and backing together. Baste the layers together as shown on page 25.

2. Follow quilting instructions on pages 25–27. Quilt on both sides of the inner borders and sashing, and outline the appliqué shapes with quilting stitches.

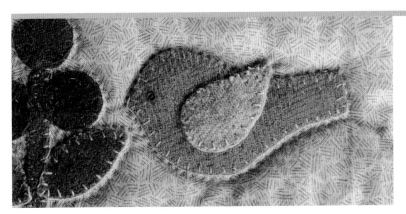

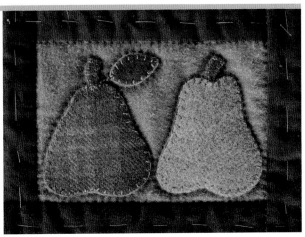

3. Stitch very close to the edges of the appliqué pieces. This will make them puff a bit and will give a dimensional effect to the appliqué shapes.

4. Remove the large basting stitches (visible on the inner border at the right) when the quilting is completed.

Binding

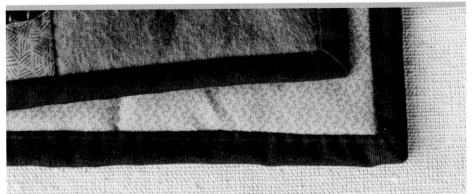

 The blanket stitch provides such a beautiful outline, it seems a shame to use thread too closely matched to the appliqué shape. A contrasting thread color adds another dimension of interest to the rich wool texture and color.

Refer to the binding section on pages 28–29 for instructions on how to piece together the binding and attach it to finish the edges of the Nature Wall Quilt.

PART III
Diagrams and Templates

The following pages provide layout diagrams and templates for each project in the book. To make it easy, convenient, and accurate for you, they are given in actual size and can be used directly from the book. The top left corner of each page is color coded and labeled for its project.

The first set of pages is the appliqué layout diagram section. These pages are used as reference for the positioning of the appliqué shapes on the fabric backgrounds. The layout diagrams are also helpful to know exactly where to place eyes, beaks, and stitching details like the curls on the sheep.

Following the appliqué layout diagrams is a section of template pages. Each template is labeled telling you what it is and what color is used. The templates are given in their actual size and are intended to be cut out of the book and used. I know that you may want to use a pattern more than once, so I recommend that after you cut it out, you place it in a small, plastic, resealable bag and staple that bag into the back of your book. Your labeled templates will be safe and available as often as you need them!

Button eye

Beak embroidered
with satin stitch

Button
eye

Embroidered legs and toes

Chicken Hot Pads
Rooster Appliqué
Layout Diagram

*Instructions
on page 33.*

Button
eye

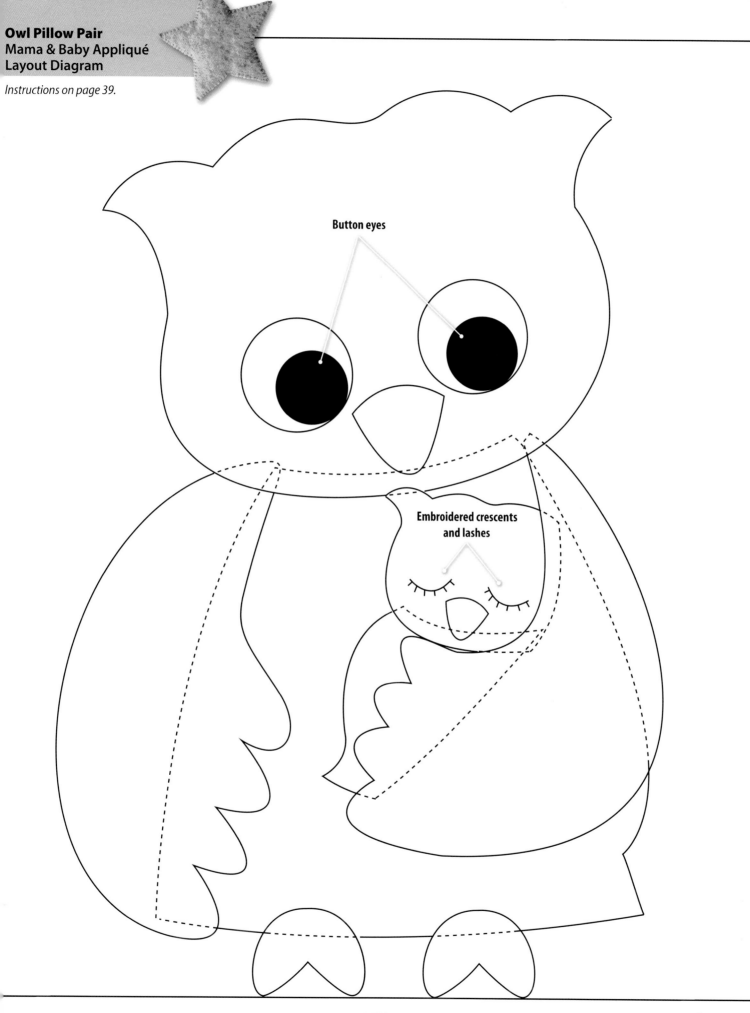

Button eyes

Embroidered crescents
and lashes

Owl Pillow Pair
Tree Owls Appliqué
Layout Diagram

*Instructions
on page 38.*

Button eyes

*Note: The pieces extend
beyond the edges of the page.*

Button eyes

Note: The tree roots overlap the pillow border.

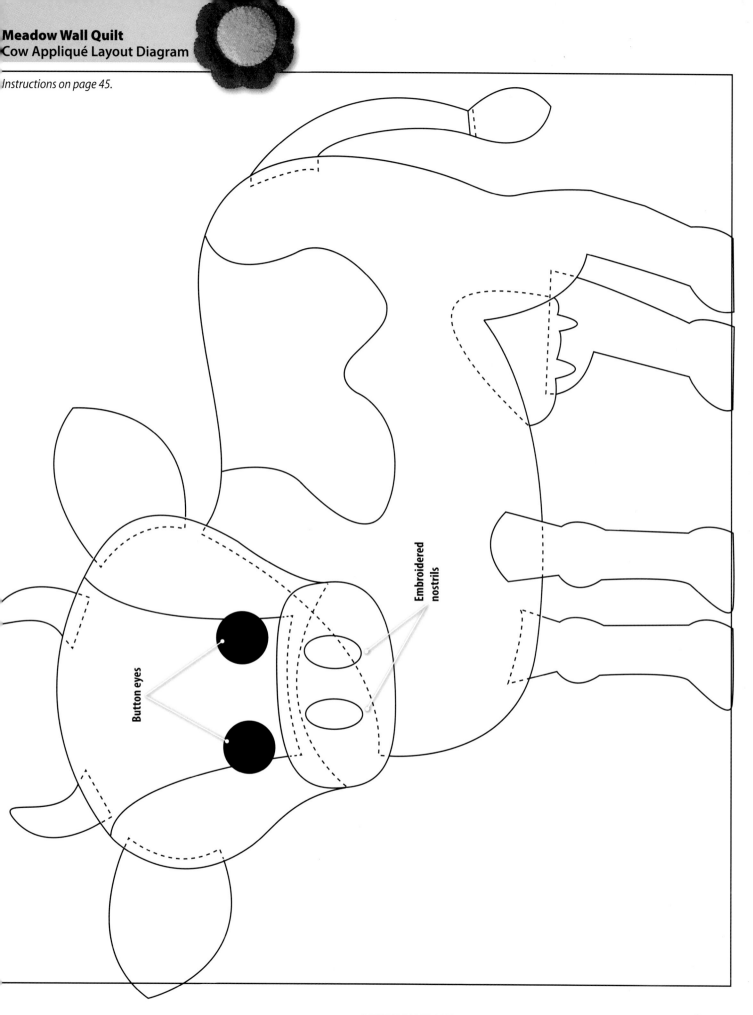

Button eyes

Embroidered nostrils

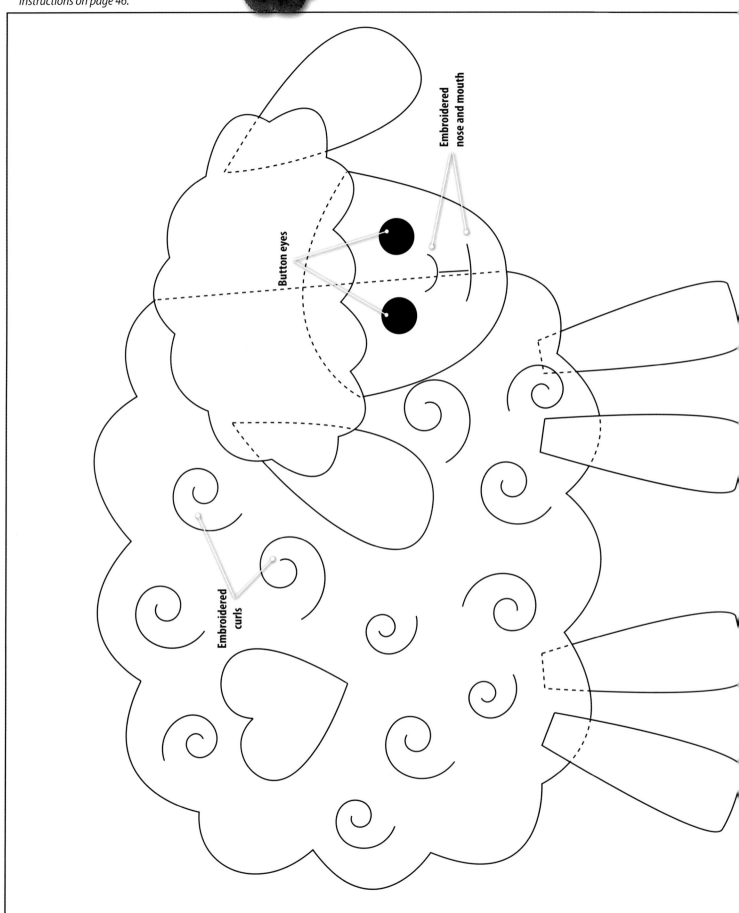

Embroidered
nose and mouth

Button eyes

Embroidered
curls

Button eye

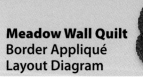

Meadow Wall Quilt
Border Appliqué
Layout Diagram

Instructions on page 48.

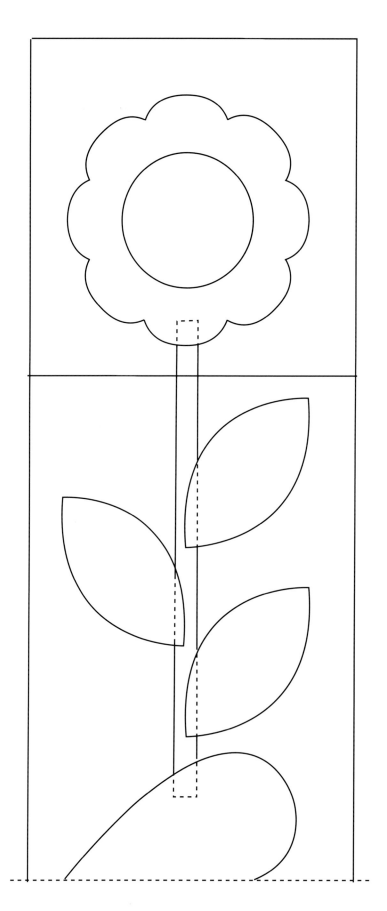

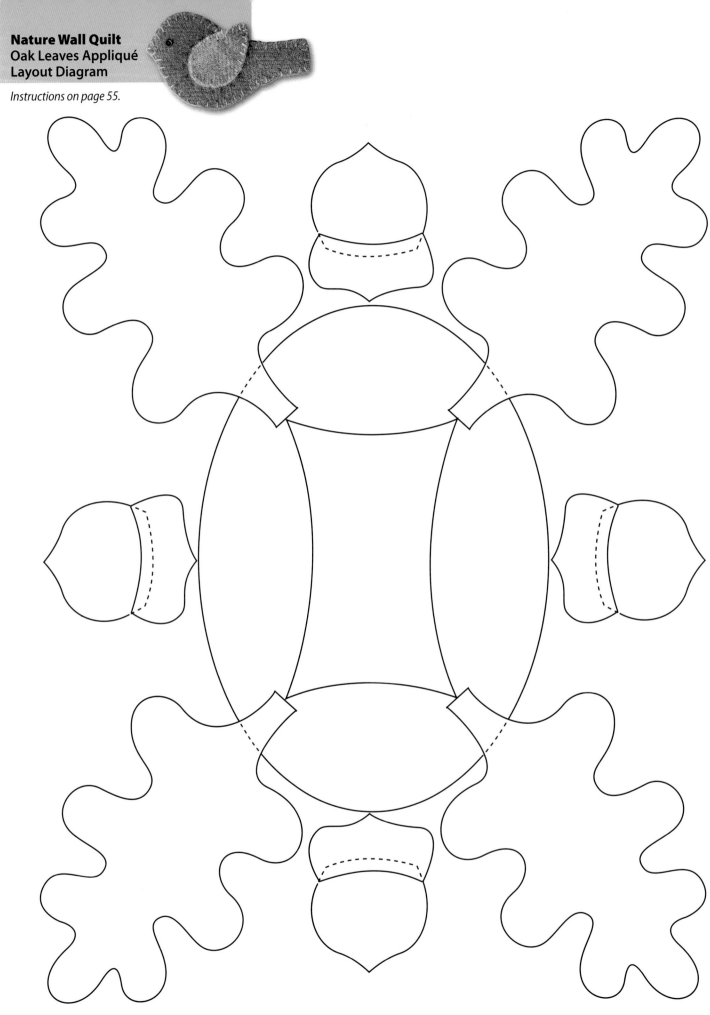

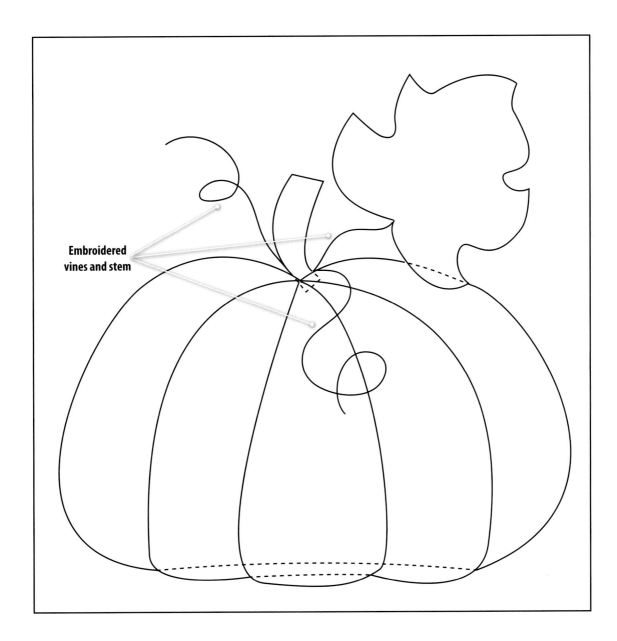

Embroidered
vines and stem

Nature Wall Quilt
Berries Appliqué
Layout Diagram

Berries Block
Layout Diagram

*Instructions on
page 55 and 21.*

Nature Wall Quilt
Pears Appliqué
Layout Diagram

Instructions on page 55.

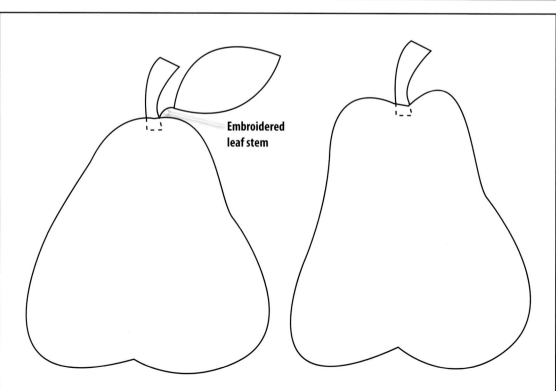

**Embroidered
leaf stem**

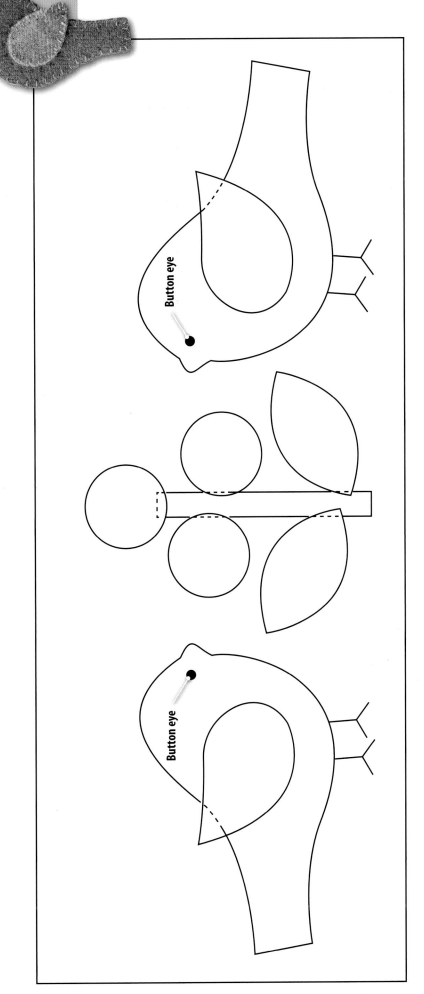

Button eye

Button eye

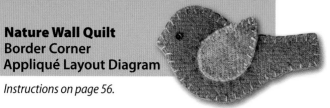

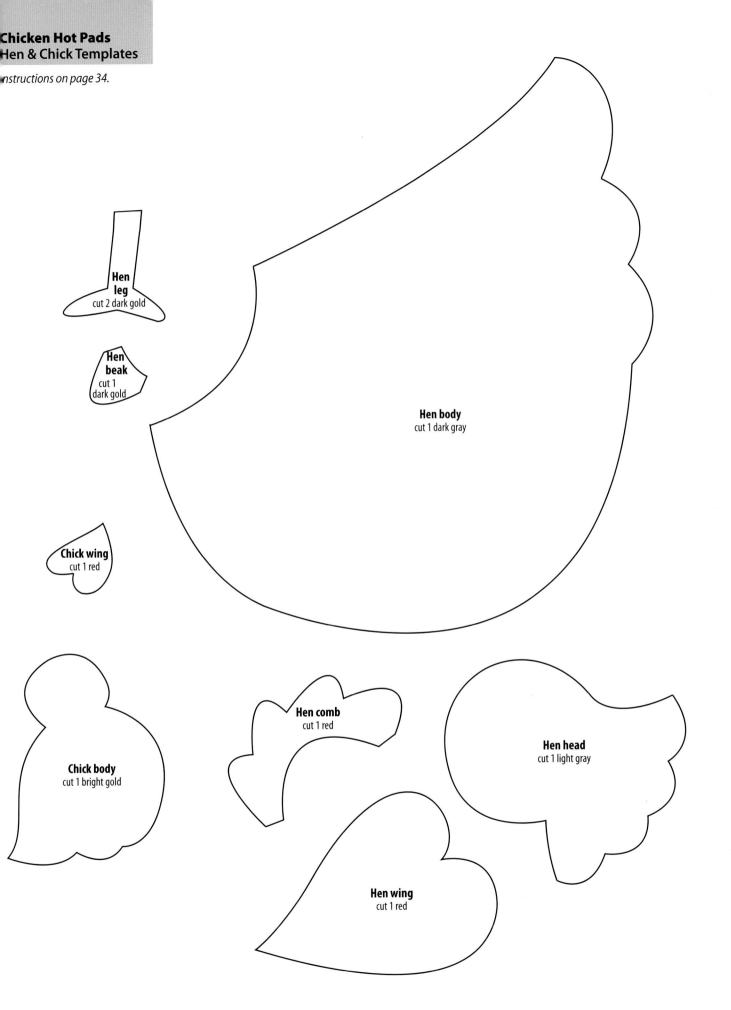

Hen
leg
cut 2 dark gold

Hen
beak
cut 1
dark gold

Hen body
cut 1 dark gray

Chick wing
cut 1 red

Chick body
cut 1 bright gold

Hen comb
cut 1 red

Hen head
cut 1 light gray

Hen wing
cut 1 red

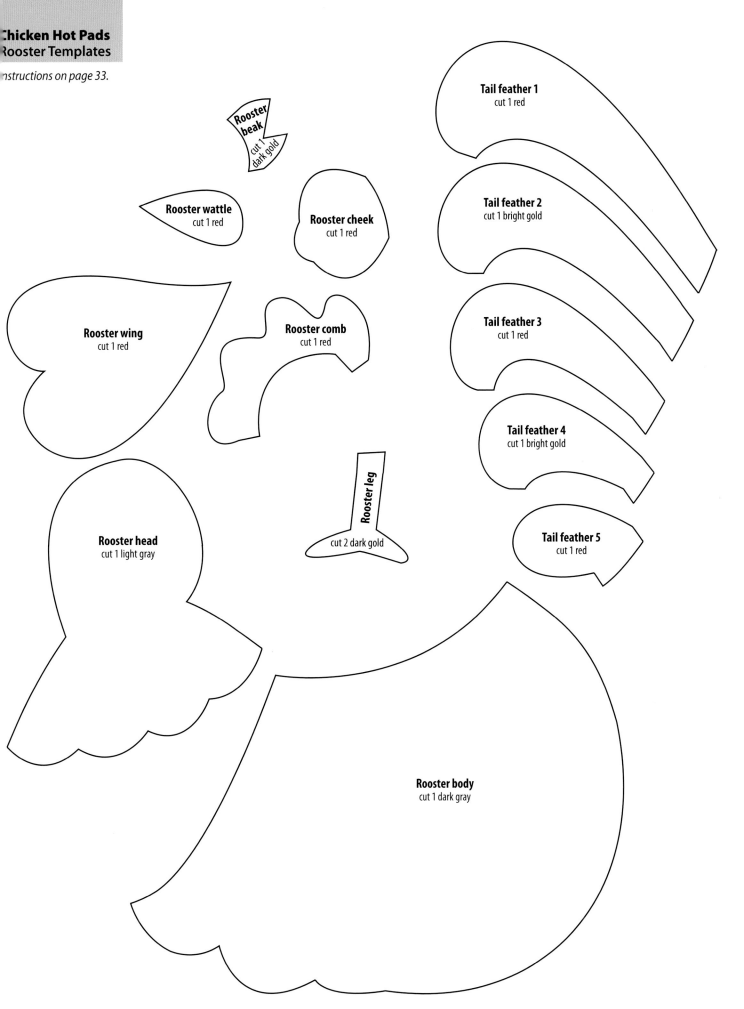

Rooster beak
cut 1 dark gold

Tail feather 1
cut 1 red

Rooster wattle
cut 1 red

Rooster cheek
cut 1 red

Tail feather 2
cut 1 bright gold

Rooster wing
cut 1 red

Rooster comb
cut 1 red

Tail feather 3
cut 1 red

Tail feather 4
cut 1 bright gold

Rooster leg
cut 2 dark gold

Rooster head
cut 1 light gray

Tail feather 5
cut 1 red

Rooster body
cut 1 dark gray

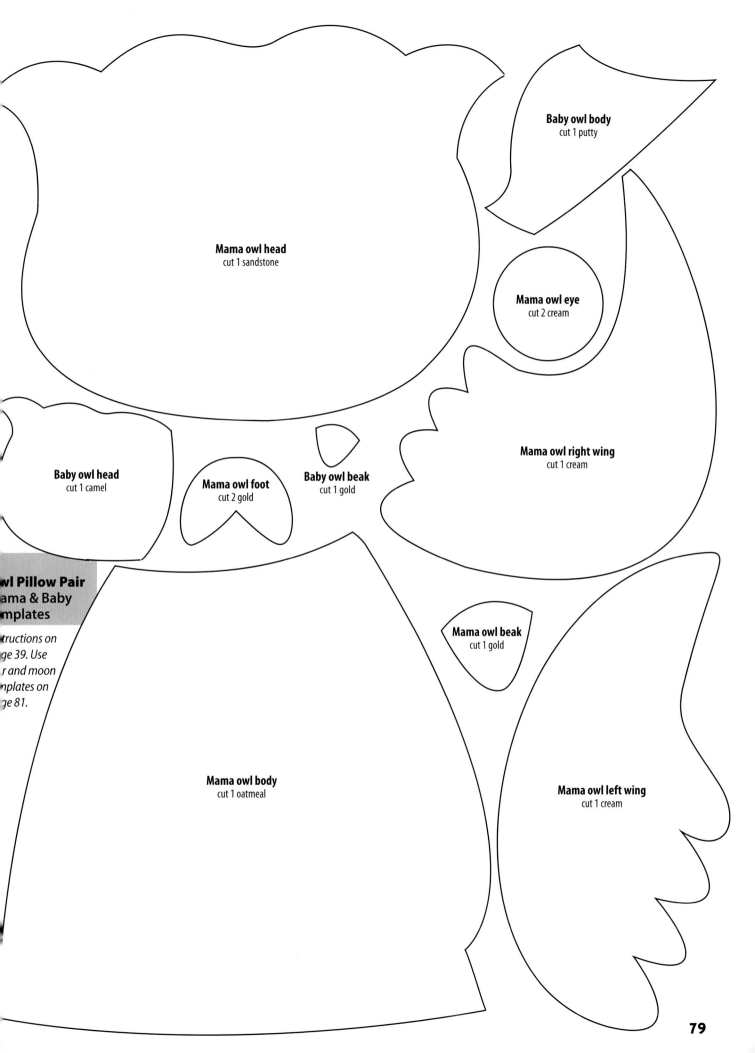

Baby owl body
cut 1 putty

Mama owl head
cut 1 sandstone

Mama owl eye
cut 2 cream

Mama owl right wing
cut 1 cream

Baby owl head
cut 1 camel

Mama owl foot
cut 2 gold

Baby owl beak
cut 1 gold

Mama owl beak
cut 1 gold

wl Pillow Pair
ama & Baby
mplates

tructions on
ge 39. Use
r and moon
mplates on
ge 81.

Mama owl body
cut 1 oatmeal

Mama owl left wing
cut 1 cream

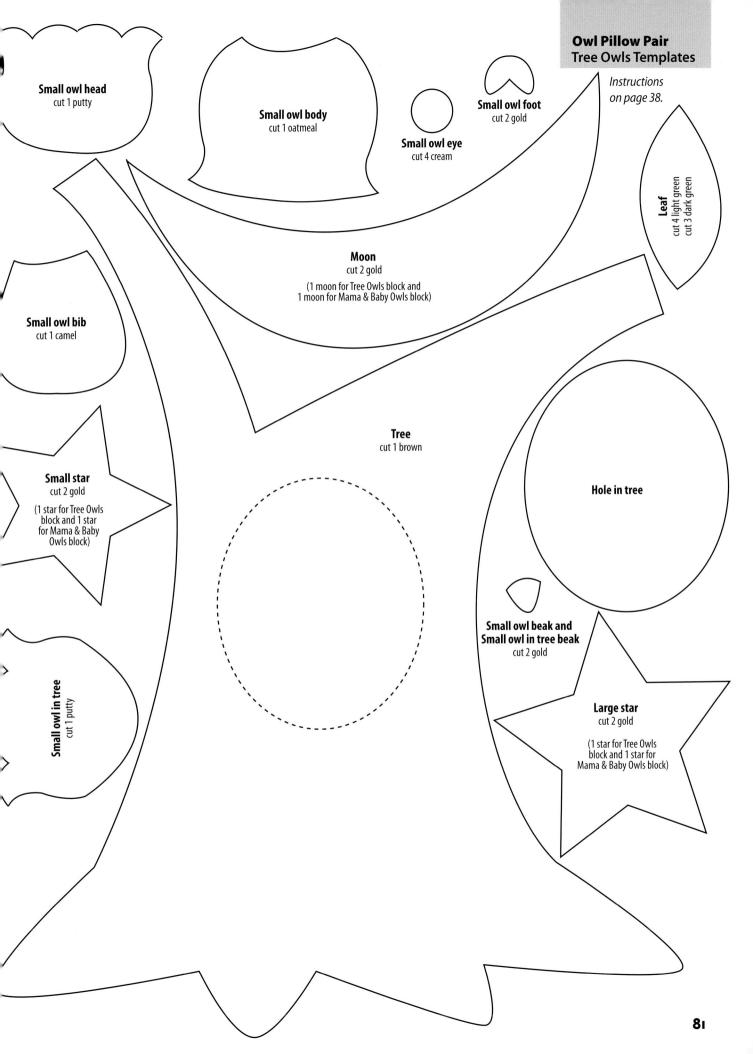

Small owl head
cut 1 putty

Small owl body
cut 1 oatmeal

Small owl eye
cut 4 cream

Small owl foot
cut 2 gold

Leaf
cut 4 light green
cut 3 dark green

Moon
cut 2 gold

(1 moon for Tree Owls block and
1 moon for Mama & Baby Owls block)

Small owl bib
cut 1 camel

Tree
cut 1 brown

Hole in tree

Small star
cut 2 gold

(1 star for Tree Owls
block and 1 star
for Mama & Baby
Owls block)

**Small owl beak and
Small owl in tree beak**
cut 2 gold

Small owl in tree
cut 1 putty

Large star
cut 2 gold

(1 star for Tree Owls
block and 1 star for
Mama & Baby Owls block)

Instructions on page 45.

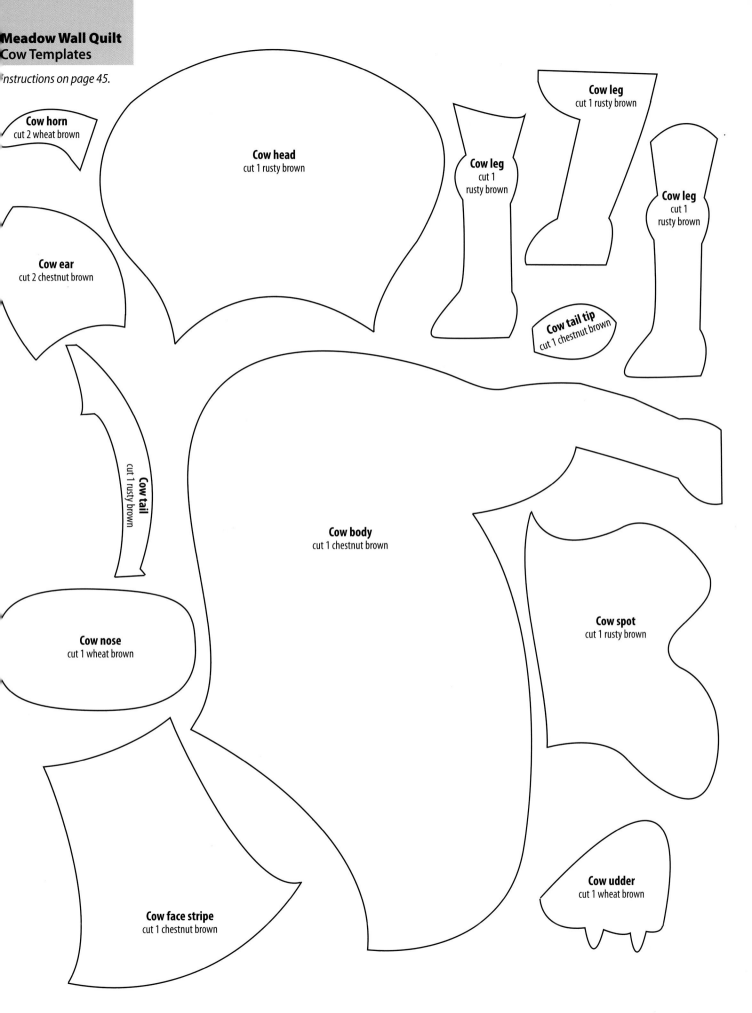

Cow horn
cut 2 wheat brown

Cow head
cut 1 rusty brown

Cow leg
cut 1 rusty brown

Cow leg
cut 1
rusty brown

Cow leg
cut 1
rusty brown

Cow ear
cut 2 chestnut brown

Cow tail tip
cut 1 chestnut brown

Cow tail
cut 1 rusty brown

Cow body
cut 1 chestnut brown

Cow spot
cut 1 rusty brown

Cow nose
cut 1 wheat brown

Cow udder
cut 1 wheat brown

Cow face stripe
cut 1 chestnut brown

Sheep head
cut 1 white

Sheep leg
cut 4
dark gray

Sheep ear
cut 2 dark gray

Sheep face
cut 1 dark gray

Sheep body
cut 1 oatmeal

Sheep heart
cut 1 red

Border heart
cut 4 red

Border flower
cut 4 red

Border leaf
cut 36 green

**Border stems
(no template given)**
cut 4 green ¼" x 6"
cut 4 green ¼" x 14"

Border flower center
cut 4 gold

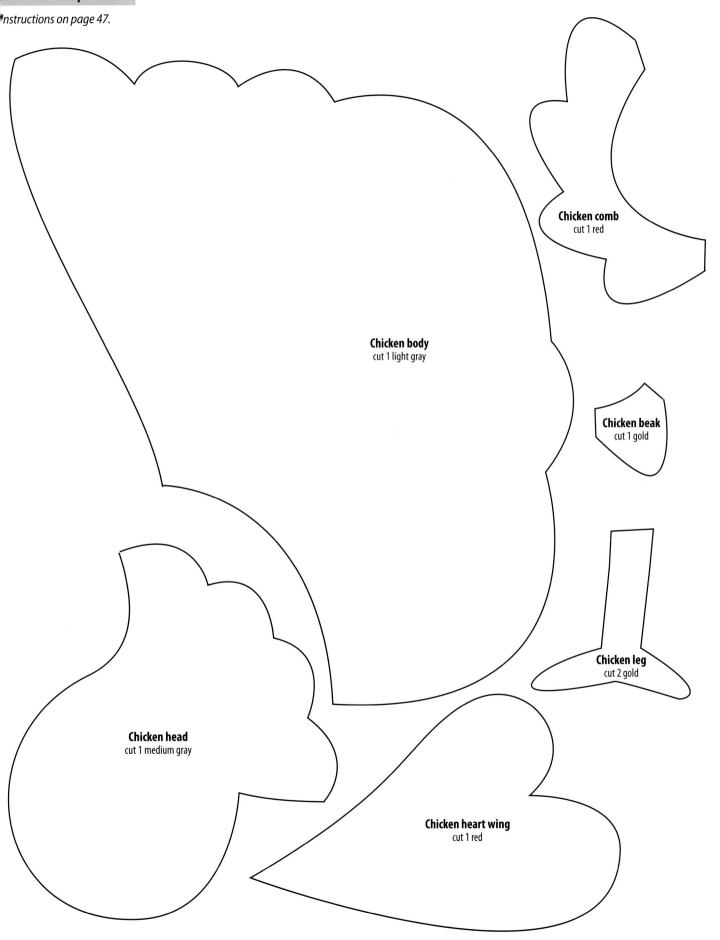

Chicken comb
cut 1 red

Chicken body
cut 1 light gray

Chicken beak
cut 1 gold

Chicken leg
cut 2 gold

Chicken head
cut 1 medium gray

Chicken heart wing
cut 1 red

Instructions on pages 53 and 55.

Oval flower
cut 4 medium red

Oak leaf
cut 2 medium orange
cut 2 light orange

Oval stem—cut 1 green

Oak leaf oval
cut 1 green

Acorn base
cut 4 dark brown

Round flower center
cut 4 light gold

Acorn top
cut 4
light gold

Leaf
cut 12 green

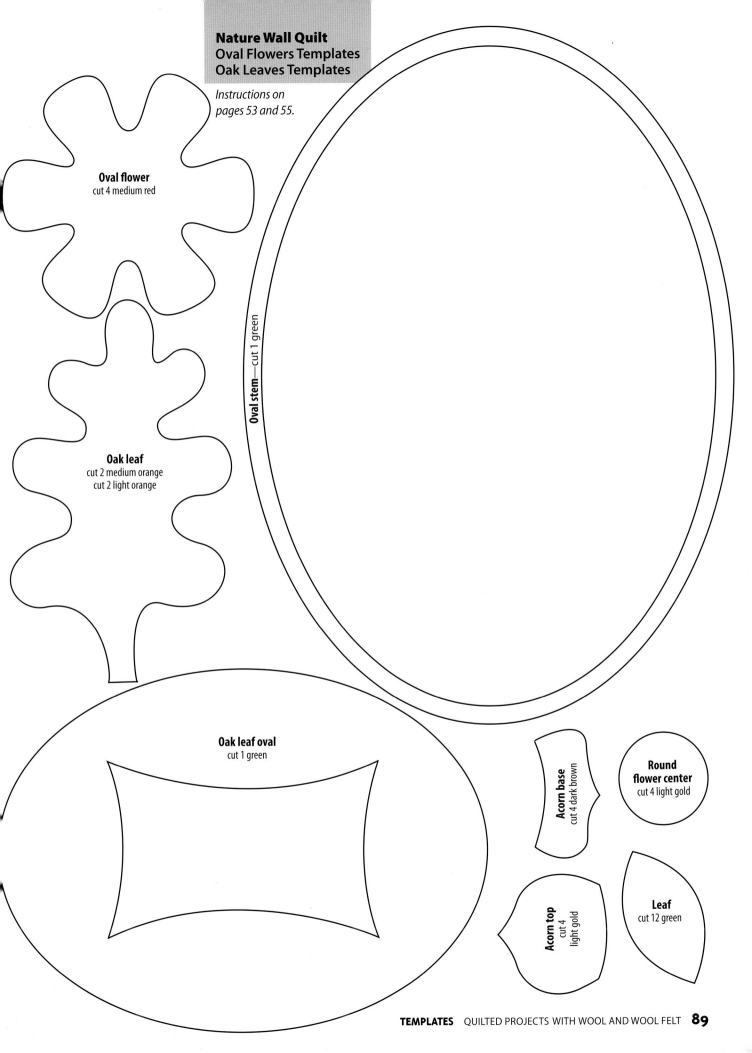

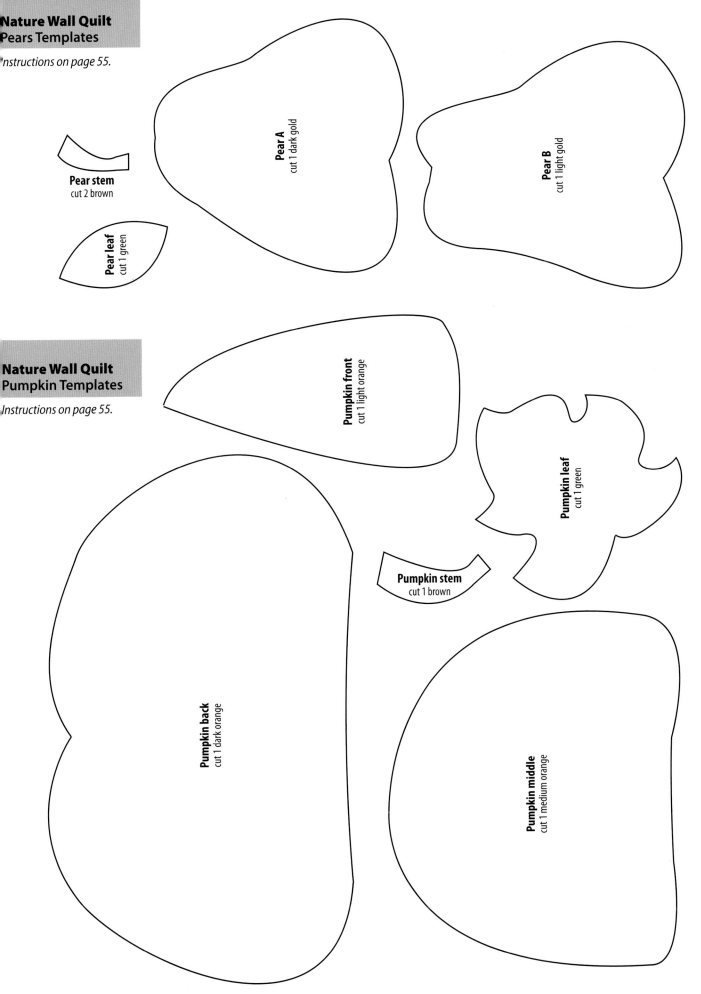

Nature Wall Quilt
Pears Templates

Instructions on page 55.

Pear stem
cut 2 brown

Pear leaf
cut 1 green

Pear A
cut 1 dark gold

Pear B
cut 1 light gold

Nature Wall Quilt
Pumpkin Templates

Instructions on page 55.

Pumpkin front
cut 1 light orange

Pumpkin leaf
cut 1 green

Pumpkin stem
cut 1 brown

Pumpkin back
cut 1 dark orange

Pumpkin middle
cut 1 medium orange

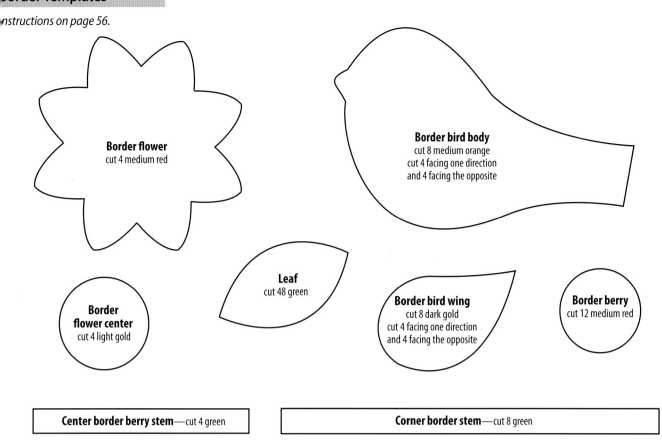

Border flower
cut 4 medium red

Border bird body
cut 8 medium orange
cut 4 facing one direction
and 4 facing the opposite

Leaf
cut 48 green

Border flower center
cut 4 light gold

Border bird wing
cut 8 dark gold
cut 4 facing one direction
and 4 facing the opposite

Border berry
cut 12 medium red

Center border berry stem—cut 4 green

Corner border stem—cut 8 green

Nature Wall Quilt
Berries Block
Berries Templates

Instructions on pages 55 and 21.

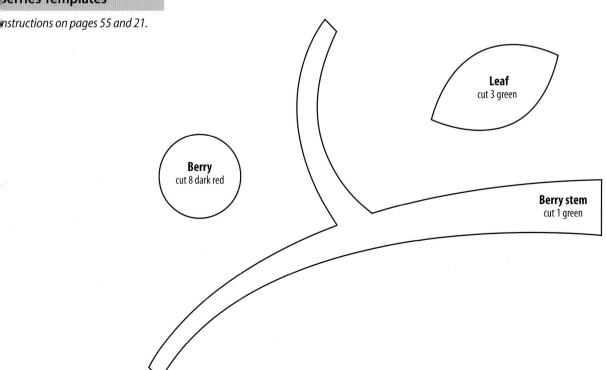

Leaf
cut 3 green

Berry
cut 8 dark red

Berry stem
cut 1 green

Glossary

Appliqué: The process of applying one fabric on top of another. The appliqué shape is laid on a background fabric and "appliquéd" in place using an appliqué stitch.

Basting: Stitches done to temporarily hold things in place. Because they are temporary, they are usually very large stitches.

Batting: The inner layer sandwiched between the top and back of a quilt. Batting gives the quilt puffiness and provides insulation value.

Binding: The finished edge of a quilt. Binding encases the raw edges of a quilt and gives it a secure, neat, and clean edge.

Borders: Strips used around the edges of a quilt. Borders act as a frame for the interior pieced or appliquéd design.

Grain: Fabric is woven with threads going both lengthwise and crosswise throughout the fabric. This is called the grain. The lengthwise grain, parallel with the fabric's selvage, is the most stable with little stretch. Crosswise grain has more flex when stretched. Fabric cut on the bias—a 45° angle from the lengthwise and crosswise grain—has the most stretch.

Piecing: Sewing pieces or patches of fabric together. Piecing can be done by hand or with a sewing machine.

Pressing: Ironing stitched seams.

Quilt/Quilting: A decorative fabric "sandwich," a quilt has three layers—top, middle, and back. The top is usually a pieced or appliquéd design. The back is often a printed or plain fabric. The middle layer is batting which provides both insulation and puffiness. The three layers of the sandwich are held together by stitches that pierce through all the layers and hold them together. These stitches are the quilting stitches.

Raw edge: The cut edge of fabric.

Rotary cutter: A tool much like a pizza cutter for cutting fabric. Used with a special ruler and mat, a rotary cutter can make very accurate and precise straight edges.

Quiltmaking ruler: A specially designed ruler for measuring and cutting quilt patches.

Sashing: Strips used between patches in a quilt top.

Seam allowance: The term used to identify the width of the seam when sewing patches together. The seam allowance is the distance from the sewn line to the raw edge of the patch. The standard for piecing a quilt is a ¼" seam allowance.

Selvage: The outer edges of woven fabric. Fabric yardage will have a selvage edge on both sides of the lengthwise grain.

Template: Another word for pattern. A template is used to trace a pattern onto fabric. Templates that are traced only once or twice can be made of paper. Professionally manufactured templates are often acrylic and are great for durability and accuracy. Homemade templates can be made using cardboard (backs of tablets or file folders), thin plastic (lids of plastic containers, the side of a soda bottle, or discarded x-ray film), or heavy paper. The important thing is that the template is very accurate, and that it be checked regularly for accuracy as repeated tracings may wear the edges.

Thimble: An apparatus to guard against sore fingers that can result from repeatedly pushing a needle through fabric. Early thimbles were most often made of metal. Today, thimbles come in a wide variety of materials and shapes to accommodate personal preferences.

*You may choose to finish a quilt block by displaying it in a frame (without glass) instead of adding a fabric binding. Shown here is my **Berries Block** (instructions begin on page 13).*

Index